When The Holy Spirit Speaks

James Bryan
When the Holy Spirit Speaks

Published by: Heir Media

Editor: A.C. Bryan

Cover Design by: A.C. Bryan

ISBN-13: 979-8-9859254-0-1

When the Holy Spirit Speaks

James Bryan

Table of Contents

Prelude   11
By Elder Craig Randolph, MBA

Foreword   13

Preface   17

The Leap   21
Chapter 1

The Authority   31
Chapter 2

His Personality   43
Chapter 3

The Teacher   59
Chapter 4

SPIRIT to Spirit   71
Chapter 5

Was That You?   83
Chapter 6

The Order We Need   93
Chapter 7

Gentle and Loving   103
Chapter 8

His Temple   115
Chapter 9

Worship In Spirit and Truth   127
Chapter 10

The Enabler   139
Chapter 11

Amen   149
Chapter 12

Endnotes   155

Prelude

Foreword

By Elder Craig Randolph, MBA

Pastor James Bryan has chosen to take on a task that many shy away from. This task is to write a book on the Person, role, and work of the Holy Spirit. I say that it is a task that many shy away from; because, from a theological standpoint, the Holy Spirit has been made to be a difficult subject to understand. Additionally, you get a different understanding depending on what environment you're in, what you are viewing, and, if you have been told about church doctrine or the Biblical role, Person, and work of the Holy Spirit. I urge you: Don't run away and leave the book, it gets better! In this book, Pastor James breaks down what could be a complex subject into bite-sized pieces, then brings it all together so that it can be digested as an entire meal.

To be a bit transparent, I have known James and the Bryan family for over 30 years. I know them so well that they are the Godparents to our now adult children. One thing that I have learned about James, is that he is a teacher—not by trade or education, but by gifting. You will see this gift distinctly in this book.

I don't want to give much away, but in chapter 1, James says, "Jesus is the greatest in taking potentially complex concepts and simplifying them for the hearer to understand." This accurately exposes who he has been modeling! Instead of wondering if the Holy Spirit is just an emotional feeling, or referred to as "a thing," or something for holy rollers, or only someone that visits when "shouting music" is played; you will learn that He (the Holy Spirit) is a Person, *and* is instrumental in each of our walks with Jesus. I ask you to take time to go through this book and study the Scriptures. When you get to the end you will not only be better for it, but you will know the One that is called to walk alongside of us.

Thank you James, my brother, my friend, my mentor, for being you, and for allowing me to play a small part in what God is doing through you.

Preface

It is with immense pleasure that I write this book.

The Holy Spirit- otherwise referred to as the Spirit of
God, the Holy Ghost, the Helper, the Comforter, and several
other names— is the third person of the Godhead; and, is
often the most misunderstood. I, like many others in the Body
of Christ, have come to know Him (and His purpose) more
personally during these recent times. Because He is precious in
so many ways, I felt compelled to share certain truths about Him
through this book.

Let me first acknowledge that I am aware that those who
read this book have various levels of Biblical understanding of
the Holy Spirit. Some, will outright deny that He exists; others,
upon learning of the Holy Spirit, would be eager to hear more.
Yet, another group of readers may have a deep theological
understanding of the Holy Spirit and the Godhead; while others
may have a deep experiential understanding. Lastly, there is
probably a group of you who just don't know what to believe.
Whatever group you fall into, my hope is this book will provide
additional— hopefully deeper— insight into who the Holy Spirit

is and His role in our lives.

Personally, early on in my years as a Christian, I had "heard" of the Holy Spirit; but I honestly didn't understand who or what He was. Was He a "force" that existed? Was He an other-worldly agent of God used to bring about His will? Was He just a theological term developed in theology schools? I didn't know for sure; and, unfortunately, I didn't have anyone around me who could provide *any* clarity on the topic.

At the church I attended when I was growing up, we often sang a hymn whose refrain went like this:

"Spirit of the Living God, fall afresh on me."[1]

I loved the simple melody and looked forward to every time we sang it, but it didn't help me understand the Holy Spirit better. Due to the frequency of this song being sung, I fell in love with the harmony of the voices in the choir more than acquiring a better understanding of who He (the Holy Spirit) is. Was He some*one* or some*thing* that hovered over us, and, at certain times fell on us? And what does *fall on us* mean? At that time, I just accepted that He existed in some form, but I didn't give much additional thought regarding Him. Instead, I focused on learning about Jesus— our Savior, His love and sacrifice for us, and His plans for our future. That, in itself, was enough for me.

Compounding my lack of understanding was the impression (given by some) that they didn't want to speak too much about the Holy Spirit. At a church I attended during my early adult years, those who wanted to understand more about the Holy Spirit were looked at as *Holy Rollers*.[2] It was understood that we should stay away from "those people;" and engrained that *we* should not be like *them*.

At one point during my membership at the church, we discovered something about the well-known (and well-liked) choir leader— her husband began to search for a better understanding of the Holy Spirit. This, of course led to him being bestowed the title of a "Holy Roller." I was amazed, although I didn't quite know what that meant. Was he going to act as if he was possessed? Was he going to begin running up and down the aisles? I'd heard of the crazy things that people did when they "caught the Spirit;" and, as you can imagine, all sorts of insane images were running through my mind. In reality, he didn't behave like a crazy man. He just shared with others what he was learning about the Holy Spirit. Eventually, he left the church and began attending one of those "Holy Roller' churches because they taught about the Holy Spirit and His role in the Church. At the time, I thought he had gone over to the "dark side," never to be seen again!

Growing up, we referenced the Holy Spirit through our hymns, but we rarely preached about Him. There were some churches that I knew of (in the same denomination as the church I attended) that were a bit "livelier." I vividly remember preachers saying, "I feel the Holy Ghost coming on me!" However, I didn't know what that meant other than the preacher was going to preach longer and with more energy. I also knew it meant lunch would be delayed. Depending on the church, it would also queue up the organ and the other instruments, followed by shouts and dancing in the aisles. Does that sound familiar to you?

Based off of those moments, I thought that the Holy Spirit showed up when the music was good and people got excited. I thought it was the part of the service that everyone waited for because the music was pumping and the pinnacle of the preacher's message would be reached. But on those Sunday's where we didn't hear the preacher say, "I feel the Holy Ghost coming on me," where was the Holy Spirit? Did we prevent Him from coming? Was there a formula that we forgot to follow? It was a bit confusing.

My hope is that you will take this book to a quiet place, read it, and consider what is being shared. Then, strengthen your relationship with the Holy Spirit. He is accessible to everyone, just as Jesus told us the Helper would come (John 14:26).[3] Let the Helper— the Holy Spirit— be a part of your life.

*J*esus answered, "Most assuredly, I say to you, unless one is born of water and the Spirit, he cannot enter the kingdom of God. That which is born of the flesh is flesh, and that which is born of the Spirit is spirit. Do not marvel that I said to you, 'You must be born again.' The wind blows where it wishes, and you hear the sound of it, but cannot tell where it comes from and where it goes. So is everyone who is born of the Spirit."

John 3:5-8[4]

The Leap

Chapter 1

As you can tell from the previous section, although I learned about Jesus and I loved Him, I didn't really understand the Holy Spirit. Some of you may be amazed at how little I understood, but I would guess there are countless others who are in the same boat that I was in during my younger years. My understanding was deficient and desperately in need of growth. If I were ever on a game show and was asked, "Who is the Holy Spirit?" I would not have known what to say. To gain a better understanding, I had to choose to grow. You see, we like to see people grow in knowledge and understanding in our academic studies and careers, but that growth wouldn't happen if there was no desire. Without the commitment to years of study and countless hours of work, degrees would not be achieved, and promotions would not be earned.

The same is true of spiritual things.

Each of us must grow through studying Biblical truths and learning from anointed preachers and teachers. Being comfortable with the basics is not always a good thing. Fortunately for me, I felt a *pulling* inside of me to learn more.

Deep within me, I felt a *need* to understand the Holy Spirit. Thus, I addressed the need by studying, praying, attending conferences, and listening to teachings about the Holy Spirit.

Before I could really grow in my understanding, I had to encounter a phase in my life that— *I hope*— everyone faces. I had to encounter something that I like to call, "***The Leap***." Let me take a moment to explain this to you. Innately, people learn through life experiences. These experiences usually include interactions with other people or the environment around us. From those interactions, we learn how to work, how to think, what is acceptable, what is not acceptable, what is safe, and the list goes on. Additionally, our experiences with the world around us, teaches us cause and effect. For example, if a child hits his sibling, that sibling will hit back, or tell their parents. Either way, there is a response to the action of hitting his sibling; or if someone yells at a stranger in an angry tone of voice, the one shouting should expect a response from the stranger. Oftentimes that response is not a pleasant one! The lesson learned should be to not strike others or treat people harshly.

Since our experiences are based on things we see and encounter, it becomes difficult for some to initially take *The Leap* when their experiences tell them a different story. For example, if Dylan was always told to keep his money under a mattress for safe keeping, but later in life a wise person tells him that keeping money under a mattress is not safe; then Dylan would look at the person with suspicion because his experiences have told him that mattresses work just fine. His experiential reality told him to only believe in what he has already had an experience with— the mattress. In order for Dylan to change his habit, he would have to believe what the wise person told him, *and* he would have to put his trust in a bank with which he had no previous experience. Change can be daunting.

The Leap requires a person to believe in Someone who they cannot see or touch at present. It also requires them to believe that much more exists than meets the eye. Additionally, it makes them acknowledge that they do not have full control over their lives. For many, this is an unacceptable and potentially terrifying concept to grasp. Again and again, from generation to generation, many wonder, "How can anything or anyone other than what I see, impact *my* life?" In fact, you may be asking yourself this question right now.

Let me give you another example. In North America, most people have heard of El Niño. If you're unaware (or possibly don't live within the confines of North America), this refers to the warmer than average surface temperatures in the Pacific Ocean that periodically occurs. As it turns out, these changes in temperature impact the weather both in Canada and the United States. Because of this, Canada and the northern United States have become dryer than normal, while the Gulf has become wetter than normal. It's hard for the average person to see the change in water temperature, but they surely experience the result of the changed weather patterns brought about by El Niño. Our esteemed meteorologists tell us these weather phenomenon exist, so of course, we take it as fact. If we believe this, why not take *The Leap* and believe the Holy Spirit is real? ***God has spoken about the Holy Spirit since the beginning of time. His effects are all around us.***

What most people forget to consider is the fact that human beings have the ability to "believe" something is possible before it comes to pass; to "imagine" a world of possibilities. A person who wants to start a business has to imagine the business, its offerings, its structure, and its possibilities before it ever comes into existence. If this is a common occurrence in the business world, why is *The Leap* so difficult?

I have heard it said that before opening a new business, you should project what you will be doing the first 30, 60, 90, and 180 days of operations. Doing this step gets you prepared and focused so your daily operations run smoothly. When you are projecting in this manner— in essence— you are taking *The Leap* as it pertains to your business. Surely, we can do the same when it comes to the Christian faith.

We all must make *The Leap*. In the book of John, there is an account of a Pharisee who visited Jesus at night.[5] This Pharisee— whose name was Nicodemis— was puzzled about how Jesus could do the things He was doing. Although he was well educated, he had never heard messages preached quite like Jesus preached, or seen miracles of this magnitude and nature. Jesus preached with authority, and all of Heaven and earth seemed to obey Him.

Instead of boldly approaching Jesus when the crowds surrounded Him, Nicodemus came to Jesus by night so that his counterparts—the other Pharisees— would not know He was curious about the "radical"message Jesus was preaching. In essence, when he approached Jesus, Nicodemis was acknowledging the fact that Jesus as a Teacher from God; but Jesus, knowing what was truly on the mind of Nicodemis, addressed the heart of the matter— he must be born of the Spirit. This came as a shocked to Nicodemis because his understanding of the Spirit of God was limited, *and* it required him to take a leap of faith to believe that what Jesus said was true. It also required him to believe in something that his counterparts did not fully acknowledge. At first, Nicodemis had difficulty processing this revelation given to him by Jesus. His reaction could be compared to a computer getting overwhelmed with instructions, and as a result, crashes. However, before Nicodemus could crash, Jesus gave him additional information to consider in hopes that he would take *The Leap*.

You see, Jesus is the greatest at taking potentially complex concepts, and simplifying them for the listener to understand. Jesus knew that Nicodemis could identify with the daily elements of nature, so He related the Holy Spirit's work to the wind. He knew that Nicodemis understood the wind existed, even though he couldn't see it. The wind is noticeable only by feeling or by observing the effects of its movements. Likewise, Jesus let him know it is the same with the Holy Spirit. Just because you cannot see Him does not mean He does not exist. He is eternal and the Third Person of the Godhead. He is mentioned from the first book of the Bible, all the way to the last chapter of the last book of the Bible.

In the past— and, to some limited extent today— you could find houses in neighborhoods with wind vanes attached to the roof. In my memory, I can see them in rural areas and farms occasionally being moved by a gentle breeze. Although they had an important purpose in the past, today they are used as little more than a decoration. In the past, they were used to assess the weather by denoting the wind direction and the speed. This helped to alert people nearby of when a storm might be approaching. By watching the impact of the wind on the wind vanes, people had to first acknowledge the wind existed, and second, they had to understand the message that the wind (and, subsequently, the wind vane) was telling them about the state of the weather. If the vane was still, the likelihood of a storm approaching was small; but if it began to turn faster and faster, it indicated a storm was approaching.

As I am writing this portion of the book, I am on vacation looking out from our balcony to the golf course below. The temperature is in the mid-80's and it is humid; but every few moments, a cool breeze comes. This is where I want to say, "THANK THE LORD!" I am not sure which direction the wind is coming from, but I am grateful for it. The breeze comes to cool things down just enough to allow me to enjoy the weather and, in turn, the environment. Bright sun, warm weather, and a breeze. It's perfect! (I did not calculate the direction of the wind, but I am more than happy that it comes). I can't see the wind, but I do see the effects of the wind specifically through the movement of the leaves on the trees. In the same way, Jesus gave a simple analogy to Nicodemis in order for him to comprehend the Holy Spirit and how He works. For the first time—maybe even the fist time in his entire life— Nicodemis realized there was so much he didn't understand. In that moment, he realized all of his years of schooling didn't prepare him for this!

Because Nicodemis' life was based on ritual, routine, and memorization, his spiritual understanding was underdeveloped until Jesus entered his life. It is the same way with many of us. We may have been "good people" for years, and have read a portion of the "Good Book," but it takes a spiritual rebirth to be part of the Kingdom of God, *and* to be who God called us to be. The Holy Spirit is instrumental in this rebirth.

I realize that many are still identifying with Nicodemis, and may even be asking, "How can this be?" I would invite you to continue to explore this topic; and as you do, I believe your understanding will increase. Many of you may also wonder:

> "How can we talk about a God—not to mention the Holy Spirit—that we cannot see?" or;

> "If I don't have a definitive understanding of how He—the Holy Spirit— reacts, then how do I know He reacts at all?"

This "leap" from physical, tangible interactions and influences, to spiritual and faith-based outcomes, is a leap many believe is too far. But the truth is, this is precisely the leap that we all must make. The leap is not as far as we might think, but it does take a willingness to make the leap.

In reality, Jesus was hoping we would take *The Leap*. He even told His disciples He was going to The Father, just so He could send the Holy Spirit to be with us and in us.[6] Jesus acknowledged the importance of the Holy Spirit in their lives and ours. If it were not so, Jesus would never had mentioned Him.

This reminds me of the well-known movie, "Indiana Jones: The Last Crusade." In the film, Indiana Jones— the titular character— encounters a deep, and seemingly endless, cavern. Unfortunately for Indiana, he needs to get to the center of the cavern in order to find the object of his adventures— the chalice. To add to his troubles, there was no bridge or ladder that could easily take Indiana across the cavern to his intended destination. Even his map suggested that he had to take a "leap of faith." He struggled with whether he should take the step because the cavern was deep, and Indiana found himself at a crossroad: If he fell, that would be the end of him; but if he didn't take the leap, he'd need never reach his goal. Instead of forgoing his goal, he decided to take the "leap of faith." Once he took the step into what seemed like "thin air,"the bridge manifested, and he was able to walk over to the cavern. In reality, this is a great example of the type of "the leap" we all must take. The more we acknowledge and pursue the Biblical truths of the Holy Spirit, the more we will grow and comprehend the will of the Lord for our lives.

So you may ask, what is the key thing we need to understand about the Holy Spirit? And why is it so important that Jesus even spoke about Him? The answer is simple: without the understanding of the Spirit of the Lord, there is no entry into the *power* that God has for us; and without that power, we can't even begin to live our Christian lives to the fullest (or even begin to achieve what God has for us). Without that understanding of who He is, there is no rebirth that can occur. Without that understanding that He provides, there is no way to really have a good and deep relationship with God. If you take a moment to think about it, you will notice that Jesus' ministry didn't really start *until* the Holy Spirit came upon him (after His baptism).[7] It was that baptism—and subsequent power of the Holy Spirit— that propelled him to do and represent God in everything that he did. In much the same way, we definitely need to have the Holy Spirit to be a key part of our lives.

When you can take that leap with me and believe that the Holy Spirit exists, then you can begin to understand other spiritual truths. The Holy Spirit is a crucial component to understanding these other spiritual truths because, as Jesus said, the Holy Spirit is here to teach us all things.[8] So, in order to be taught, we have to acknowledge the teacher. If we acknowledge the teacher, then we are in a position to receive the teachings. If we receive the teachings, then we will be able to understand more of what God has in store for us, and our lives will be changed.

It is important to know that The Holy Spirit does exist. He is the Spirit of God mentioned at the beginning of Genesis.[9] He is the Comforter[10] that Jesus promised to the Disciples that He would send. He loves us, and everything He says and does points to what Jesus taught. He knows the heart of God, and the depths to which God loves us. He is here to guide, teach, and strengthen. He is the very Spirit of God.

Will you take "*the Leap*" with me?

*B*ut the Helper, the Holy Spirit, whom the Father will send in My name, He will teach you all things, and bring to your remembrance all things that I said to you.

John 14:26

The Authority

Chapter 2

I'm glad that you have decided not only to take "The Leap," but to take your understanding of the Holy Spirit a step further by reading this chapter. Fantastic! Now that we've covered the basics of why the Holy Spirit is important, we can now begin to dig deeper into other aspects of the Holy Spirit. For example, His authority.

The Holy Spirit is nearer to you, than you may realize. In fact, regardless of whether you believe He exists or not, He is next to you while you are reading this book. One of His qualities is He is omnipresent.[11] That means He is everywhere—exists everywhere— at the same time. In other words, there is no place He is not. In every meeting, every restaurant, every country, every home, every office, every school, the Holy Spirit is there. There is no hiding from Him. Even if you paid the large sum of money to be one of the first explorers to land on Mars and build a settlement, the Holy Spirit would be there. It doesn't matter where you run or hide, He is there.

Since He is everywhere, some of you may ask the following questions:

1. If He is there, does He care about everything that occurs in my life?

2. If He is there, does that give Him the right to interfere or examine all my life's activities?
3. What gives Him the authority to be everywhere at all times?
4. If He is there, why doesn't He just do what He wants and change everything in my life?

These are all great questions, so let's take a moment to examine the Holy Spirit's authority.

When it comes to God, authority and order matter. Nothing can exist unless God allows it. We also know that God follows the rules that He established; therefore, the Holy Spirit must be here under God's authority *and* for a purpose. Let me explain it this way: Each of us exists within a country (whether or not we belong to the same country does not matter for this example). Most people would agree with this statement. If your country wants to show goodwill to another country, they would send an Ambassador to that other country. The Ambassador is given the authority to represent your country, since the authority was given to him by the leader(s) of your country. Additionally, the Ambassador sent to the other country for a purpose, or else the government would not send him. His purpose is to represent your country, and improve relations between the two countries. The Ambassador has both authority and purpose.

The same is true with the Holy Spirit. He represents God. He, as the Spirit of God, knows the *will* of God in order to adequately represent God. He is fully qualified. He has seen everything from eternity past, all the way to the present. He definitely has firsthand knowledge!

He was there in the beginning[12] when everything was created. He has been involved in the events and affairs of mankind all throughout man's development. He is aware, and knows the plans for the future. Additionally, John 14:26[13] tells us that the Holy Spirit is sent from God the Father in Jesus' Name. That gives Him the name and authority to be here, since the name of Jesus carries the only authority that is higher and more prominent than any other name that exists. Therefore, there can be no question as to whether the Holy Spirit is here legally and by authority. If He is "sent" from God the Father with the authority of Jesus, that means He must have a purpose. A person is only sent when something needs to be accomplished. That begs the question: what does the Holy Spirit need to accomplish?

If we stop to remember that Jesus came to the earth to bridge the gap between God and mankind by providing a path to salvation, and He— the Son of God— came in the form of Man to pay the sin-debt so that we all can have the choice of salvation; then, salvation essentially means eternal life through Jesus Christ. Once everything was accomplished, the Holy Spirit was sent with a purpose. That purpose was to teach and bring to remembrance all of the things Jesus taught to a world that was lost and separated from God. The reason for this is Jesus' words provide light for salvation to anyone who believes. In other words, the Holy Spirit points us to Jesus. By pointing us to Jesus, he is essentially bringing us to the bridge that takes us from judgment to eternal life.

Now, let's expand upon an example I used earlier in the book. When I spoke about hearing preachers say, "I feel the Holy Ghost coming on me," I came to realize what they were trying to express was the active involvement of the Holy Spirit in directing the focus of the service— including the preaching. On many occasions, I have witnessed the Holy Spirit redirecting the flow of the service in order to answer a need or question of a specific person. He did, and currently does this to let that specific person know— without a shadow of a doubt— that Jesus cares about them. This personalized message usually draws people to the Bridge of salvation, which in turn, results in eternal life through Jesus.

This reminds me of a memory I have of a young lady who became part of a small group that my wife and I were leading. During one of our meetings, we spoke to the group about hearing from God. We discussed that God does speak to us in today's time— usually through the Holy Spirit. The young woman mentioned that she had never heard God speak, but she was intrigued by the possibility. Her face lit with wonder and excitement about the possibility that the God of the universe would actually speak to a person such as herself; however, I could also see she was struggling with how and *why* God speaks to us. She had never been taught about this before. My wife and I explained that she could simply ask to hear Him speak, and that she would know it's Him because He will not say anything contrary to what is written in the Bible. By the end of our small group meeting, she made the decision to take "the Leap" and stepped out in faith, asking God to hear His voice. She didn't hear God's voice at that very moment, in fact, a period of time passed— roughly three to four weeks— in which the topic did not come up. However, during one of our Sunday morning church services, I saw her sitting several rows behind us (my wife and I happened to be in the second row); during the offering time— and after she came to the front to give her offering— she walked back to her seat, but not before briefly looking at me with a big smile and saying, "I heard God's voice for the first time!" The glow and the joy on her face was amazing! She was so excited since the message impacted her directly. That encounter let her know for sure God existed, and it propelled her to study the Bible even more.

I want you to know the Holy Spirit will communicate with you—wherever you are— in order to introduce you to The Savior, Jesus Christ. The Holy Spirit will even explain the Word of God to you, if you let Him. It is through the Word, coupled with the Holy Spirit's explaination, that will guide you through life, your relationships, your business decisions, your marriage, and more. The Holy Spirit has the authority to make things happen. He knows that you are loved (according to John 3:16[14]), and He wants to make sure that YOU understand the depths of the love poured out for you.

Knowing the purpose for which He was sent, and having a pure understanding of the love God has for us, the Holy Spirit is focused on teaching us all things and bringing to remembrance the things Jesus said. His mission is to declare Jesus to all who would listen—but He will not force you to accept him. While He knows that a relationship with Him is what you and I desperately need, He also acknowledges that it is ultimately our choice.

Now, some of you have probably asked why He hasn't made Himself known without question? Why doesn't He speak throughout the globe with a loud voice, saying, "I am here?" Well, from God's viewpoint, it is obvious that He exists based on every created thing that exists around us: nothing appeared by accident. There are too many variables to allow for an accidental creation. At a minimum, He expects us to realize that someone greater than ourselves created the world and the universe. When we think about how great, intricate, and vast creation is, it should bring us to a general awareness that God exists. From there, He begins to work; letting us see who He is through the lens of the Bible.

When I think about Jesus' original Disciples, I realize it must have been a time of unknowns, of being scared and being excited, and having their emotions run haywire. They witnessed supernatural events, and experienced revelation about scripture that they had never heard before. Jesus would often proclaim truth to them, but it took further explanation for them to truly understand. In one example, Jesus told them that he was going away,[15] and that it would be *better* for them that he went away; or else the Father would not send the Helper. They were probably wondering what he was talking about, but Jesus explained, once He left, the Helper would be sent to each one of them. Essentially, describing the purpose and nature of the Helper (the Holy Spirit). In this discourse, He was letting the Disciples know that everything was going to be alright, and the One that He would send would be with them, guide them, and empower them. He would come in the authority given by Jesus.

Whenever I listen to someone speak on a particular topic, I tend to focus even more when I know the speaker has personally experienced what it is they are discussing. There is truly something special when listening to someone who has "been there and done that," versus someone who speaks purely from theory. Because they have the experience, it lends to their credibility; however, it doesn't always mean that I agree with everything they say. For example, if I listen to a sports radio host, I'm more inclined to believe their commentary if I know they have actually played a sport. When they talk about a sport that they have played, there is enthusiasm and their real world examples provide a clearer image of the topic.

A couple of decades ago, I went to a conference to hear a preacher minister about the Holy Spirit and hearing His voice.

I put a lot of credence to what he said because I had seen him working *and* operating in that area. Since I was still searching and trying to understand what and who the Holy Spirit is myself, I was interested in hearing from someone who had experience. During his message, partway through, I could feel something changing inside of me. Excitement began to build inside of me as I was being filled with the nutrition that I needed. Every word he spoke felt as if he was teaching directly to me! My insides were doing "flips," and it was becoming harder to contain my excitement. I thought I was going to erupt in a shout. The mere idea that I might erupt in that manner frightened me since I was, at the core, an introvert. The challenge was, I could not control what was happening inside. Even though this was what I had been asking for, I didn't know how to handle it when the experience began.

There were many people at this particular service, but it seemed so personalized— as if he knew my questions and what I was seeking. Truthfully, I know that he didn't know who I was or what I was seeking, but I later realized that the Holy Spirit did! The Holy Spirit had the authority to address my questions and fill my need because Jesus gave it to Him. It was critical that my heart was open to receive what the Holy Spirit needed to share with me.

When the service was finally over, I was exhausted. I just sat there thinking about the things the Holy Spirit was sharing with me and how personal it felt. I now had my own personal experience with Holy Spirit.

Experience does matter in our journey in better understanding the Holy Spirit. That is why I think it's important to listen to the Holy Spirit, because He has experience. First of all, He is the spirit of God. That means, He knows the heartbeat of God. Additionally, He understands the will of God. The Bible says no one can understand the will or thoughts of a person except the spirit of a person.[16] The same is true with God— because He is God and understands the will of God, therefore what He says must have credence. We must also realize that He has seen everything that there is to see from eternity past all the way to today. If he has seen all things, then He must understand the entire plan *and* what is needed for each and every one of us to thrive. He has the credentials because He has "been there and done that." If any other spirit or being suggests that they know everything that has ever been done, then it has to be a lie. There is only one Holy Spirit. He is the only one that exists from eternity past to eternity future. He has authority.

Another question that you may be ask is, "How long does the Holy Spirit retain His authority?" That's a good question! For starters, the Bible *does* tell us the duration, or length of time, that the Holy Spirit has authority given to Him. In fact, the Bible is very specific in answering this question. Jesus even spoke about it when he told the Disciples that he was going to send a Comforter. During that discourse, Jesus shared that the Holy Spirit would come, and that He would abide with us *forever*. Forever is a long time; so much so, that it never ends. Jesus spoke first to the disciples, then that word was shared for all who would believe. That means, anyone who would believe Jesus' word today will also have the Holy Spirit in their lives. The Holy Spirit has authority that never ends; so He will continue to work in your life today, tomorrow, and forever— if you allow Him.

Now let's address one of the common challenges that everyone faces at some point in their relationship with— or their seeking of— the Holy Spirit. Although He has authority, He won't force that authority on you. He will work in you, and he will work through you, but only if you allow Him. God has given all of us free will; and He wants us to choose Him rather than force Himself on us. Although He abides in everyone who is born again (through salvation) through the name of Jesus, He will only reveal as much truth as you allow Him. The more you want to receive, the more revelation He provides; but, He is one, as a person, that can be grieved. He wants to share so much about who Jesus is, and what He has done for us, that it grieves Him when we reject His revelation and instruction. He has all authority to show us the immeasurable Truth and guide us according to Jesus' word. He wants us to experience the enormity of grace that Jesus has given to us. When we reject Him and what He wants to share, it greatly disappoints Him.

Like Jesus, He does not want us to experience life without the Lord. With that said, should you decide to let the Holy Spirit actively work in your life, keep in mind that since his authority comes from Jesus, you cannot invoke the Holy Spirit without first being saved by the Lord Jesus, the Savior.

If you ask why someone wouldn't allow Him to work in their life, it would be because they would not want to surrender their plans, relationships, power, and things to the Holy Spirit. Many people are attached to what they think they have or earned, so they do not want to relinquish control over it. You have to hand over control—coming with a seeking and a willingness to be instructed— to grow this relationship. Simple examples of people being attached to "their life" are as follows:

1. Anyone who has risen to a level of importance that they do not want anyone adjusting or interfering with how their time is used. Every moment of their time is spent with people they think are important. If the Holy Spirit wants some of their time, He is "penciled in" at the bottom of the list, if at all.

2. Someone who has plenty of things (clothes, money, food, etc.) but they are not willing to give to those that are in need— even when the Holy Spirit instructs them to do so.

3. In general, people who are focused on themselves, who are not willing to surrender and let the Holy Spirit show (and do) much more in their lives.

4. People who will not believe or entertain the thought of the Holy Spirit, even though He is referred to throughout the Bible. Their traditions, or their lack of desire to seek the truth, have limited their ability to receive what Jesus has already established. The Holy Spirit, without question, is here as a benefit not a detriment.

It is extremely important to receive what Jesus gave. In other words, Jesus wanted all of us to receive His salvation then live life more abundantly! So how can we live life abundantly? We live an abundant life by following God's commandments, which the Holy Spirit will highlight and explain to us. That's His purpose and his pleasure. Living an abundant life that is everlasting, beginning right here on earth, is His desire because it is Jesus' desire.

*B*ut the fruit of the Spirit is love, joy, peace, longsuffering, kindness, goodness, faithfulness, gentleness, self-control.

Galatians 5:22-23

His Personality

Chapter 3

This is one of my favorite topics when it comes to discussing the Holy Spirit. In order to truly understand, you must get past the idea that the Holy Spirit is a force or a thing. That concept is *so* far from the truth. In fact, that type of thinking will make it difficult for you to believe the Biblical truth about the Holy Spirit. But I know, since you have gotten to this chapter, you truly want to know the truth about the Holy Spirit.

When addressing His personality, it can seem like an enormous task. Just think about it for a minute—we are talking about the one involved in the creation of the universe; the one who always was, always is, and always shall be; we are talking about this spirit of God. The one who was involved in designing everything in such detail that we need supercomputers just to begin to understand the vastness and the complexity of all creation. He's the one that created celestial objects that are so much larger than our own planet, and lifeforms that are so small that we need special devices— such as microscopes— to notice them. The vastness and the variety of what He's created is inumerable; and yet, we seek to have an understanding of His personality. How can we begin to understand His personality when many of us have trouble understanding the personalities of our neighbors and our spouses? How do we relate in such a way that we can begin to understand and describe His personality? Well, I have a few ways and a few descriptions that may help you in your understanding.

He is a person that you truly need to know; and yes, I did say a person. In order for me to tell you more about the Holy Spirit as a person, you need to understand more about what the Bible says about Him.

The Bible verses mentioned at the beginning of this chapter reference the fruit of the spirit. The fruits of the Spirit are the results— or evidence— in the lives of Christians who spend time with the Holy Spirit; and these evidences cannot be prevented from showing up in the lives of Christians. The fruit that is mentioned in those verses are actually manifesting from the Holy Spirit's actual personality. For example, you cannot have apples produced from any other plants, except an apple tree. An apple is the fruit of an apple tree. That is what it is. It is not the fruit of an almond, or even an orange tree. Likewise, you cannot have oranges coming from any thing else but a tree that produces oranges. A tomato plant does not produce oranges. A key point to remember is that the fruit of something points back to the nature of the originator. In other words, fruit is the result of the personality and "being" of the originator.

With that understanding, we realize the fruit of the Spirit is an indication, or a view, into the personality and qualities of the Holy Spirit. The good thing is, we can count on these qualities being a stable foundation of our relationship with the Holy Spirit. Therefore, we can "know" Him and His personality, because the characteristics are laid out for us in the Bible.

I am not going to give you a textbook definition of all nine fruits of the Spirit, as there are many resources to provide that information. Instead, I plan to layout examples from real life encounters that should help you understand more about His personality, and the result of spending time with Him. As I so often say, He is precious and here to help you through every aspect of your life. He is dependable, or else the Lord would never have sent Him. He is caring, or else he would not be the Spirit of God.

The Bible refers to love being a fruit of the spirit. I want to caution you, *and* help you understand that this kind of love is not a lustful love or desire. It is a pure love not based the thought that someone earned it, but based on grace.[17] It is the love that Jesus demonstrated for us on the cross, and is found in the Holy Spirit who offers it to each one of us. This love transforms and impacts people's lives today.

Several years ago when we lived in another city, we had small group meetings for our church in our home. Initially, the small group meetings consisted of just a few people; but not long after the initiation of that particular small group, the attendance grew exponentially. Since those attending the small groups ended up bringing their families, we had more people than the definition of a small group would allow. Since those attending brought their family members, we did not want to split them up. To remedy this, we ran multiple small groups from our home at the same time. We had a group that occupied our family room, another group occupied our living room, and yet another group that occupied our basement. This did not include our church's other small groups that were taking place at different homes and locations around town. There came a point, though, when we couldn't house all of the people in our home. However, when we approached some of the small group members in order to encourage them to attend a small group in a different location, they did not want to comply because they were able to feel love in at this home and this location.

I must tell you that what they experienced was the presence of the Holy Spirit. It was an outpouring of His personality. Because we abided in His presence, the small group experienced many deliverances, encouragements, successes, and revelations. The truth is, it really had nothing to do with me or my wife; it was the presence of the Spirit of God that ministered to the heart and souls of everyone who attended. That was a powerful example of his love being poured out, because love is at the core of His personality.

Let me give you another, although similar, example. When it became time for us to sell our home and move to yet another location, we placed it on the market. During this time, people came through the house with their real estate agents to inspect and decide whether they wanted to purchase the home. Some of the those people who toured the house later left comments telling us that they felt love and a special warmth in the home. In fact, the couple that purchased the house because of the love and warmth they just felt in that home. These people were not necessarily Christians, but the love of the Spirit of God permeated down to the buyers who fell in love with that place. The love they experienced was due to the presence of the Holy Spirit who abided there, because my wife and I learned to spend time with Him. In other words, because of the habitual time that we spent with Him, His presence was made known to those who entered the doors. Due to that— and numerous other experiences— I am very familiar with this aspect of His personality.

In addition to His love, I have discovered even more about His personality the more I seek Him. He is joyful, even sometimes joking with me. I have had numerous conversations with other Christians that will attest to the fact that there have been times in their conversations with the Holy Spirit that He will joke with them; oftentimes, catching them off guard. This is usually welcomed by them, as it brings joy and laughter— a great asset in further developing a *relationship* with the Holy Spirit. Now, I am not saying that the Holy Spirit's job is to be a comedian, but I am saying He often communicates in a way that causes laughter and joy at the appropriate times.

This is not the only way joy can be manifested in. Decades ago, I used to know a lady named, Mrs. Walker. She was wheelchair dependent in order to get around. At that stage of my life, I attended a local church that did not have an elevator. When you entered the church, you had steps that would either take you up to the sanctuary, or down to the lower level where the classrooms, the multipurpose room, and kitchen were located. One Sunday, Mrs Walker decided that she wanted to come to church. She came with her grandkids (she had wheeled herself down the street, towards the church, over broken and busted sidewalks). It's worth mentioning that in the neighborhood where I grew up, there were sections where the sidewalks would be disjointed, and malformed. There would be a couple of slabs of the sidewalk that might jut up in the air; while some may be caved in, and others may be may have been non-existent. In other words, the trek just to get to church was not easy one, and many people would rather not take the chance while in a wheelchair. Yet, it was over these sidewalks that Mrs. Walker had to manually maneuver with her wheelchair. She could not afford a motorized chair, so she had the basic wheelchair. However, at that moment of her life, she was determined to start attending church, and she wanted her grandkids to have that experience also. Therefore, on Sunday mornings, she would leave her daughter at home while she took the grandkids to church.

When Mrs. Walker arrived at the church, everyone was faced with a dilemma: "How could they get her to the sanctuary?" Additionally, how would they get her to the lower level if she had to use the restroom? However, when she made it to the church, she did something amazing. She told everybody not to worry about helping her up the stairs (she could not use her legs at all); instead, she lowered herself onto the cement floor right by the stairs, and pulled herself up— one step at a time— only using her arms to pull herself up until she reached the sanctuary level. She did this in her Sunday attire; yet she was so joyful that she could attend church, and she would not allow anything to prevent her from taking part— not even a perceived disability. The only thing she asked, was for someone to carry her chair to the sanctuary level so that she could get into it when she made her way up the stairs. What a testimony!

Everyone in the church stopped in amazement as she pulled herself up the stairs. Her determination was so intense, that it took a lot of convincing to get her accept the help of guys who were more than willing to assist her. However, it didn't bother Mrs Walker since she was where she wanted to be. From there on— each week— once she got to the top and she pulled herself into the wheelchair, she went right into the church service. The smile and the joy was beaming from her face was contagious; she had her grandkids next to her, and enjoyed every moment.

This method of attending church continued Sunday after Sunday because she knew she wanted to be in the House of the Lord. The joy that came over her for being in the presence of the Holy Spirit, was amazing; and it encouraged other church members to not complain about their situations, and to always remember how important it was for Mrs. Walker and how she pressed through. The joy that she felt— and was subsequently expressed through her determination— was truly because she got to know the Lord, and the Holy Spirit. That joy was an outcome (or a fruit) of the Holy Spirit's presence; and, it was made evident in her life from that moment forward. She would always thank the Lord for everything that He had done for her; causing her to be joyous no matter whether it was raining, hot, or cold outside. Her desire to be in the presence of other believers to worship the Lord at church. The realization of that goal resulted in shouts of joy and happiness.

The Holy Spirit brought so much joy to Mrs. Walker, that it impacted her whole family. She would speak of the presence of the Holy Spirit, not only to the church members, but also to her family. As time went on, more and more of her family began to attend church as well. Her joy was contagious! Because the Holy Spirit knows how contagious joy is, He shares that part of His personality so that it will be contagious for whoever else comes across your path.

If you thought that His joy is wonderful than you'll love the peace that the Holy Spirit provides. In the world we live in today, there is plenty of anger and hatred and frustration; but very little peace. When you read comments on social media, you can feel the anger and skepticism written in frustration in every comment section. When you receive comments like that, it may even feel like those negative emotions are reaching through your screen and hurting you; but the great thing about the Holy Spirit and his personality, is that He impacts you or pours in you peace that is beyond all understanding. He will give you "peace in the midst of a storm." He will give you an assurance and a peace that everything is going to be OK. As you develop your relationship with Him, you will never hear Him frantic as if He doesn't know what to do. He may be insistent at times, but never frantic. He brings you peace *and* allows you to calm down.

On many Thursday nights as part of our current church ministry, we have virtual prayer that is open to anyone who calls in at the appointed time. Over the course of several years of doing this, we've garnered a solid group of regular attendees. During the course of praying together regularly, they have all gotten a better understanding of this relationship with the Holy Spirit. Soon, we began to have attendees from up and down the East Coast, as well as a few on the West Coast; and many of those who attend virtual prayer had not attended church on a regular basis. As time went on, they began to feel the presence of the Holy Spirit and his draw for salvation and recommitment through Jesus; but something else also happened during that time. Many began to experience peace occurring in their life, and they realized it was spending time in the presence of the Holy Spirit of God during that virtual prayer time. For many of them, they desperately moved their schedule around so that they could partake in that virtual prayer time on a regular basis. This prayer time transformed the chaos in their lives, the raging thoughts in their minds, and their indecisiveness about what to do next in life. That newfound peace calmed them down enough to make wise and Godly decisions, and to surrender to the Lord.

Outside of our scheduled virtual prayer time, I frequently received phone calls and emails from various individuals who want me to pray with them; and, usually each person asks for one thing— peace. They each desire that the chaotic noise in their life would quiet down, and that they would have peace in order to live and breathe. Each time, I urge them to get closer to the Holy Spirit. It is in abiding with Him, that they eventually discovered that peace was actually a personality trait of the Holy Spirit. That peace allowed them to face another day; that peace allowed them to keep their head up and have hope. That peace prevented some from doing illegal acts, and some from even ending their life. That peace that the Holy Spirit shares is life changing and so important.

The Holy Spirit has a way of bringing peace into a room, a home, a church, a business, or any other place that we invite Him into. When he shows up, peace is part of what is manifested. I've witnessed scenarios where people who may be agitated, upset, or angry, "all of a sudden" calm down— to the point of becoming docile or ameniable with those they were just arguing with. What happened? The Spirit of the Lord residing in that place or on that situation is what happened. A result like this could happen because of someone's prayers, or their very presence (inspired by the Holy Spirit's presence in their life). You may even walk into some churches with a feeling of agitation and confusion; but, when you walk into a church that knows the Spirit of God, you feel— and sense— peace. This is a real phenomenon that exists. Maybe you've never taken the time to notice, but going forward, I invite you to begin to be sensitive to His presence and His impact.

This reminds me of an evangelist originally from Texas, but he would spend his time in Mexico where he would operate as an evangelist. Once a year, he would come back to the US to preach and visit churches in order to raise funds to continue to provide for the people to which he ministered. When I met him, he was in his mid-60s. He was the type that would walk around singing hymns all day long, and he would often with the Bible in his hand. He frequently spoke about his Ford Explorer which, at that point, he had for many years. Since he lived dependent upon the donations of others, his Ford Explorer was everything to him. Even though it was very old at that point, he would get all the repairs done once a year when he came back to the States. Because he had such a unique personality, I usually found myself being the one that would help and support him while he was in town. I was fascinated with him because no matter what was going on, he always had joy. The conditions in which he lived in while he was in a small rural village in Mexico, were not ideal; but he wanted to be in the midst of the people he was called to minister to. That meant that he had to endure the same hardships, and live as they lived. There were many years of lack and struggle within the ministry, but yet he continued on; and through the hardships he realized that God was faithful.

Through his experiences, he got to know the Spirit of God; and as he began to understand more of the Spirit of God, joy became the basis of his life. It was an everyday occurrence.

Peace also became a foundation stone in his life. That meant that even when aggressors came to the village where he stayed, he did not fear because he had the peace that only the Holy Spirit can provide. As he shared some of those stories with me— stories that would make an excellent movie— I would look at him in amazement; yet he would always laugh, and tell me he always depended on the Lord for his very life. There was no need to fear. Even as he was getting older, he was still depending on the Lord for the sake of the people that were around him. It was that peace that allowed him to continue to work as an evangelist with the limited resources that he had. It was that peace that allowed him to not be fearful when aggressors would come and try to steal from and intimidate those to whom he ministered. It's through that peace that he knew that everything would be alright. This type of peace is what the Holy Spirit shares with all who would spend the time to get to know him. What about you?

If you need a biblical example, let me share one from first Samuel, chapter 16[18]. In that chapter, we discover that David is being anointed king by the prophet Samuel. Although it took several years before the manifestation of the anointing (David being king) would occur, things immediately began to change in David's life. When he was anointed, the Spirit of the Lord was upon him. In contrast, it is also noted that the current king, Saul, had the Spirit of the Lord depart from him. In this account, we see that king Saul was tormented by an evil spirit; so much so that he asked for his servants to find a man who was skillful in playing an intrument to help subside the torment. If you read that chapter carefully, you see one of his servants telling him that there was, indeed, a skillful man who had God with him. It is that spirit, who is the Holy Spirit, that the servant is referencing. That Spirit is the one who gives peace. If you continue reading through that chapter and others, you will notice that whenever David played, peace was in the room. The very thing that continuously tormented king Saul had no choice but to subside when David was in the room and playing. Through David, the Holy Spirit brought peace to that tumultuous, and even toxic, environment while David was playing. It is the One that we call the Spirit of God that changes an entire environment. Peace is His fruit— a tangible outcome— which is shared and experienced only in His presence.

Jesus mentioned that for those who love Him, He would send a Helper that is very much like Him. The Helper— the Holy Spirit— is sent to assist or advocate for everyone who is a believer. If He is helping, assisting, counseling, or advocating for you, it means He cares about your outcome. He wants to see the success in you that reflects the price Jesus paid to make you free. I have personally experienced these characteristics of the Holy Spirit, and I've come to know that He is exactly as Jesus described Him. Some of you may have also discovered this in your Christian walk, but others may not have had that experience *yet*. If you have not, then I am excited for you! I am excited because I am anticipating the joy and peace that you will experience from your encounter when it happens. It will be special! You will learn so much the closer you get to the Holy Spirit; whatever you do, cherish that relationship and don't neglect it.

The Bible even talks about the Spirit of God having the ability to be grieved.[19] If He can be grieved, then that means that compassion must exist in Him. That also means He must care for and love each and every one of us; and it is only through His love, that you can truly feel grieved when something, or someone is not doing what is expected. This personality trait is something that shows His heart towards each of us.

So how can the Holy Spirit be grieved? Let's briefly talk about it. Without getting into too deep of a theological discussion, let me explain something to you. Jesus sent the Holy Spirit so that He would be there with us always. His role is to be, and stand, alongside of us; and to always remind us of the promises of Jesus. In order for Him to remind us, He must be able to communicate with us. If He is able to communicate with us, then He must be able to have some type of personality and thought process in order to communicate with us effectively. It's in that communication that we understand more about His personality.

His communication is always aligned with the words Jesus spoke, and the words that are in the Bible. They will ***never*** be aligned with anything other than what is contained in the word of God. If it aligns with his Word, then that's how you know that it truly is the Holy Spirit that is communicating with you. He is so great at communicating that He knows how to get His point across by using the methods He knows you will receive.

There have been times during prayer— and during the course of the regular day— that He has spoken to me in such a way that I've had to double check to make sure it was Him. The reason why I was surprised, was because he had a humorous flair in the way that he communicated to me. He knew that I needed to be yanked out of the cycle of rehearsing issues and instead, believe the Lord. You see he is able to communicate to all of us in the dialect, vernacular, and language that we are accustomed to communicating in. Thus, He is able to get across the *true* meaning of each conversation that He has with us.

Since the Holy Spirit communicates so well, and he knows that we have heard what he has communicated, it does grieve him when we consistently ignore His direction. He so longs for us to get the most of what Jesus has given us, that it is a major disappointment when we choose not to receive. He will try over and over again— like a loving parent, grandparent, or great teacher— to get us to listen to His wisdom; however, He knows that, ultimately, the decision is completely in our hands. Even the Bible tells us not to grieve the Holy Spirit. The reason why it is such a sticking point is because it is a declaration that we are resisting the will of God, and, in turn, the Spirit of God. If we resist the Spirit of God, how can we know the will of God? When we reject His direction and His encouragement and His leading, we are fully rejecting the will of God. That in itself will grieve the Holy Spirit because He loves each of us. It is His desire that we receive the blessing and love of God, and reject the curses and evil that come from being outside of His will.

Let me mention one last thing about the Holy Spirit's personality. Since He loves us so much, He exposes His heart to each and every one of us. Anyone who has ever been truly in love, realizes that in order to truly love, your heart is always exposed. Whenever a relationship doesn't go well, or something negatively happens to the loved one, our heart is hurt. We feel for them because we're so close to them. You can never love without exposing your heart. That's what the Holy Spirit does. He exposes that vulnerable part of himself because He loves us so much. Always remember that the Holy Spirit is functioning in love because He is the spirit of the Lord, and the spirit of God.

The Spirit of the Lord shall rest upon Him, the Spirit of wisdom and understanding, the Spirit of counsel and might, the Spirit of knowledge and of the fear of the Lord.

Isaiah 11:2

The Teacher

Chapter 4

I remember it as clear as day. When I was at a ripe age of 13 years old and in 8th grade, I began attending middle school in Howard County, Maryland. At the start of the school year, I had to make my schedule for the 8th grade. All of the required classes were selected and approved, but I still needed to select an elective class. After a little thought and encouragement from a teacher, I chose music. From what I heard, this particular class was going to be fun. The teacher was very popular among the students, so I thought this was going to be great. One of the benefits of this class was it would teach me the basics of how to play the guitar. I always wanted to learn, but I never had the opportunity; then suddenly, the opportunity arose. In my mind, I thought this would be awesome!

During the first half of the semester, I learned many wonderful things about the guitar, plus the basics of how to play. We all learned chords and how to strum them together; since we were all in the class, I thought no one could tell that I didn't truly understand everything about playing the guitar. However, one day, I noticed that a number of the students in the class had some prior experience playing the guitar. All of a sudden, I felt as if I was the only one who had never touched a guitar prior to the class. There was even one point in the semester, where the teacher announced a project that each of us would have to do. The project was one where we had to write a simple song, put a melody to it, and play it in front of the class. Not only did we have to play, we also had to sing the lyrics. At that moment, horror entered my whole body. I began to realize that by being in front of the class by myself, everyone would know that I had no idea how to play. The teacher may have noticed the terror on my face— and a few other students too; because I can remember him encouraging us, telling us we could do it.

I don't remember how much time our teacher gave us to write the song, develop a melody for it, and rehearse it in preparation for our performance; but although there was much time was allotted, it truly did not seem like enough. I know I spent almost seventy-five percent of the preparation time agonizing and visualizing myself failing in front of the entire class. By the time the day before I had to perform came, I was a wreck. You see, I had never written a song. In addition to that, I had never created a melody to put with a song; and, to make things worse, I barely knew the chords on a guitar, so I had no idea how to put all of this together in less than 24 hours. This made me reach out to my sister— who was very creative— who helped me create a song for my class. This impromptu collaboration resulted in one of the silliest songs ever created! Then, after a little bit of more time, we figured out what chords would go with the lyrics. From there, I had to try to play, sing, and remember everything. I don't think I slept that well that night.

Finally, the day of reckoning arrived. As we drove to school, I held my guitar tightly, but my body was full of nervousness. When my father dropped me off at school, the walk from my father's car to the front door of the school seemed like it was miles long when in actuality it was only a few feet. On that particular day, I had several classes prior to my music class. As you would imagine, I could not focus on the other classes— physically I was in them, but mentally I was somewhere else. When it came time for my music class, I walked as slowly as I possibly could. I remember entering the music room and sitting towards the back of the class; hoping and praying that time would run out so I would *somehow* be able to get out of it. Unfortunately, that wasn't the case. In a supportive way, my teacher called me to the front. My classmates encouragingly clapped their hands, but inside I was terrified. As I sat on the stool in the front of the class to begin to sing and to play, I shared with everyone the name of the song. Since it was such a silly song, we had to give it a silly title. When they heard the title, everyone looked at each other, chuckling. Finally, with a deep breath— and remembering how encouraging my teacher was— I began to strum and sing. I just let it out, without staring at anyone in particular. When I got to the end, I just knew I had failed. Instead, I was met with enthusiastic clapping and cheering from the entire class. I later found out that I received an A minus on that test. I was shocked! Someone who had no idea what he was doing, was able to pull off an A minus. The encouragement of the teacher and his insistence that I could do it, was what propelled me to complete the assignment. Just in case you're reading this, and want me to perform the song for you, don't hold your breath!

In the same way, the Holy Spirit is our teacher. He teaches us to do new and wonderful things. In addition to what a regular teacher does, He also empowers us to do what He is trying to teach us. The wonderful thing about the Holy Spirit is that He is able to teach us in a way that we can easily grasp what He is saying. He truly makes it plain. When we take the time to receive—and meditate— what He is saying, we can make beautiful music. Have you ever tried to understand something, but for whatever reason, it never made sense? Have you ever prayed about getting understanding, and then at some point, the understanding comes? When the understanding comes, it seems so simple. In fact it may even make you wonder why you did not understand it earlier.

At my job a number of years ago, I was in charge of a multi-million dollar project. It was a project that was highly visible, and had a *very* public deadline. Halfway through the project, a major development occurred that I never saw coming— it was a change in the foundation of the solution.

Because of this major change, the entire project success was heavily in doubt; and I was the one on the hook for delivering this project. When all these changes occurred, all I could do was say, "Holy Spirit what shall I do?" As I was going through the analysis of the project, and reviewing the options, I continually just prayed for the Holy Spirit to show me what to do. Not long after I began to pray and ask for direction, instructions came to me little by little. Each instruction He gave me, led me to what I needed to do at that moment; and, as I embarked on those instructions, another set would come shortly thereafter. It was as if I was following a trail of bread crumbs. Although it did take an immense amount of work, I did end up meeting my deadline with several days to spare. I can tell you that I probably prayed more during that time period, than at any other point in my life.

Through this ordeal, I got to know the Holy Spirit as my teacher. In order to solve the problems that were at hand, I needed more information than I had in front of me. That is the reason why I began to pray for a solution and a strategy. The Holy Spirit, as a wonderful teacher, knew how much I could grasp at any period of time. Therefore, He gave me the information I needed step by step. If He had given me the complete strategy all at one time— based on my stressed state— it would have been too much for me to handle. Therefore, He gave me what I needed, as I needed it.

Some of you may be wondering how He unveiled this information to me? Well, that is a wonderful question, and I'm more than happy to answer. First, I had to understand that the Holy Spirit works in me continually. Then, I also had to understand that there was no limit to what God can do. Therefore, I trusted and believed that the Holy Spirit— whom Jesus said would teach us all things— could surely teach and show me how to be successful even in my work. When the issue first arose on the project, everyone around me (the client as well), looked extremely worried. They understood how significant the change was, and they had no solution. When the project was delivered successfully, everyone celebrated even giving each of us, pats on the back. I appreciated the celebratory environment and the attitudes, but I was just so thankful that the

Holy Spirit guided me in such detail, all the way through to the end.

Is my experience is Biblical? The short answer is, yes. In fact, I would not share this example if it was not Biblical; but just to be sure that you understand, let me pull an example from the true source: the Bible. Do you remember the apostle Paul?[20] In the book of Galatians, Paul outlines his rise to apostleship, and details how he was able to be taught the things of God. He mentions that no man taught him any of it, nor were there other apostles who taught him. Instead, he noted that he learned by revelation. As you now well know, he is referring to being taught by the Holy Spirit. During those times of growth, when no one even knew who Paul was, he was being taught daily by the Holy Spirit. Although it doesn't explicitly say it, I would imagine that his training consisted of reading scriptures and praying; then the Holy Spirit would reveal understanding to him. He probably also had to spend time unlearning the incorrect doctrine that he had been taught for many years. This way, he was being taught directly from the heart of God. When the appointed time came, he began to share the truth of this revelation from the Holy Spirit. When considering the account of the apostle Paul, you must understand that in order for him to receive the depth of understanding that he possessed, he had to have spent large amounts of time being taught by the Holy Spirit directly. In addition, the Holy Spirit had to correct Paul's improper understanding about what he had been taught from his youth. Prior to Paul's encounter with Jesus on the Damascus road, and prior to being taught by the Holy Spirit, Paul had lived his life memorizing scriptures and believing that good works were the way to please God. The Holy Spirit had to change that whole concept.

When I think about this story and my personal interactions with the Holy Spirit, I am convinced the Lord has humor! Let me clarify what I mean. If you're already familiar with the apostle Paul's nature, then you would know that he was a very religious person, intently focused on Jewish traditions. This singular and narrow-minded focus caused him to look down on Gentiles, yet the Lord sent this type of individual to minister and help the very people he held prejudice against. It is a testimony in itself that through the Lord's direction, Paul was able to overcome his prejudice to become the one who lived with the Gentiles and be a vehicle to their salvation. The Holy Spirit had to teach him to discard his prejudices and love those he didn't formerly love. In other words, the Lord used Paul to build the Gentile portion of the church. That's why, when I look at this story, I am always amazed at how the Lord uses people. God really does have a sense of humor!

While I have been in ministry for many years and have been a Christian for many more years, and have seen my relationship with the Holy Spirit has grown tremendously; I understand that I still have a long way to go— even now. Every day, I find myself reaching out for guidance from the One who was sent to teach us all things. Early in my maturity, I would only seek guidance on very specific, or complicated, things. I fell into the trap that many also fall into: that small things are not important to the Lord. Therefore, I didn't ask the Holy Spirit to teach me, or to reveal, what I need to do. However, there would come a certain point in my life, where the Holy Spirit revealed to me that even the smallest things are important to Jesus. From that point forward, I began to share— and still do share— all aspects of what is going on in my life. As I share these things with the Holy Spirit and ask direction on areas that I don't understand, I receive answers. It reminds me of the scripture that says, "you have not because you ask not."[21]

What about you? Have you ever taken the time to ask the Holy Spirit for revelation on the will of the Lord in your life? Have you ever asked Him how to plan your budget? Or how to properly raise your children? Have you ever asked Him how to interact better with your friends and family? These, and countless other topics, are fair game in your conversation with the Holy Spirit. Don't be ashamed. Just ask and listen. Remember, there is no place you can go that is too far away from the Spirit of the Lord. It is not like an AM/FM signal, that can fade in and out. You have complete connection at all times as a born again child of God.

When you think about the different teachers you've had

over the course of your life, there are always a few that stand out. They may be memorable because of their style, the subject matter, or their impact on your life. I have had some teachers who have inspired me to do much better than I ever thought I could. Contrastingly, I've also had some teachers who have caused me to lose interest in a topic because of their poor teaching style. For example, early on in my life I had an interest in chemistry, however the teacher I received for that class was extremely no nonsense and was not one who would spend time explaining new concepts in depth. I was in that class for about a week during my high school years, only to decide it was time to drop that class for a different one. Fortunately, my counselors were able to switch me to a different class which was much more understandable. I was glad that I didn't try to stay in the class— and probably not succeed— just because I was not able to grasp what the teacher was saying.

When you interact with the Holy Spirit, you begin to realize something about Him that is both beneficial and reassuring: He understands how you learn. In other words, He speaks in a way that you can understand. Therefore, the way that He speaks to me maybe slightly different than how He will speak to you; but the words and the concepts are still the same. He is also able to make complex issues, simple. He knows how to break down concepts, ideas, issues, and thoughts down in digestible chunks in order for us to absorb what He's saying. Additionally, He knows the right mixture between visual teaching, audible teaching, and impressions. I will talk a little bit more about those areas later in the book.

If you remember, at the beginning of this chapter, there is a reference to Isaiah. I love this book for many reasons. Not only does Isaiah reference the Messiah, who from his standpoint was still to come, but his accuracy is amazing. When I look at the verse contained at the beginning of this chapter, I see something here that is very applicable to what we are discussing. You see, Isaiah is describing the Holy Spirit in verse 2. I do realize the whole focus of this passage in Chapter 11 is about the Messiah, but we get glimpses of who the Holy Spirit is in this chapter also. The passage shows the Holy Spirit being called the spirit of wisdom. If He is wise, *and* has the wisdom, then we must go to Him for instruction. Much like we go to scholars and teachers, we have to go to the One who is assigned to teach us all things. His purpose and desire is to make sure that we learn. This learning is not memorization only, but wisdom, infused with the revelation only the Holy Spirit can provide. This allows us to use the information we learn, correctly.

There are many organizations that pride themselves on their ability to collect information; but what I have learned, is information, by itself, is not beneficial. Information, coupled with the wisdom and revelation on how to use that information, is what matters. Companies who are able to take a vast amount of information, make sense of it, and apply it, are often successful. There are many companies who can gather information, but aren't able to make sense of it nor apply it. Those companies are not successful.

The Holy Spirit is much the same way as someone who is able to collect the information, discern its meaning, and apply it. That's where the wisdom comes into play. In many cases, wisdom implies that you have the ability to share insights and understanding; and coupling that with a perfect sense on how to teach, the Holy Spirit is the ultimate teacher. This verse lets us know that He is full of wisdom *and* understanding. It lets us know that He is overflowing with wisdom, and is able to share insights with us. What better way to solve a problem than to ask the One who knows all things? What better way to understand and receive revelation then to ask the One who provides it?

That same verse also goes on to say that He is the spirit of counsel. That means that you can ask Him and He will give you direction, advice, or counsel. You can ask questions that— to you— may seem silly, but He is more than willing to provide you with the correct answer. You should feel free to ask Him, "What should I do?" He is the one that will advise you on the right path, according to the will of God for your life. You can't go wrong when you include Him in every aspect of your planning and your learning.

Finally, the scripture talks about Him being the spirit of knowledge. That allows me to believe that all knowledge sits in

Him. In other words, much like how a hard disk searches for the information on its drive and then presents it, He is able to go and provide information on any topic, from any time or place, and give it to you. Insights that even your superiors may never grasp. However He can give it to you— and give you the understanding on the matter.

Let me give you a simple example. Think about the disciples that followed Jesus. None of them were scholarly people. The only exception may have been Matthew, who probably was very good at math; the others were very ordinary people. After Jesus' resurrection, and after the disciples received the Holy Spirit, they began to understand and preach about the scriptures and promises of God in a way that no scholarly person had. So much so, that their knowledge surpassed that of many of the scribes and Pharisees. How did they get that information? Did they all of a sudden take a crash course to learn everything? No. Jesus had put the seed in them— the truth. From there, the Holy Spirit came and illuminated the truth that Jesus had placed in them, teaching them how to connect the truth in order to see the whole picture. That is why they were able to preach about the meanings of scriptures, that prior to, were not understood correctly by the teachers of that time. That is why the Holy Spirit is here, and that is why I tell you that part of His personality is to teach. He wants to show you the vastness of the truth that is out there for each and every one of us.

Will you allow Him to teach you? I'm not speaking of limiting Him to teaching you just certain things in your life. I'm not even asking you to limit Him to giving you revelation only on a Bible verse. I am asking you to allow Him to teach you *all* things. That means all things relating to life and godliness. If you will allow him to do that, I guarantee that your life will change for the better.

Now when they saw the boldness of Peter and John, and perceived that they were uneducated and untrained men, they marveled. And they realized that they had been with Jesus.

Acts 4:13

SPIRIT to Spirit

Chapter 5

I don't know about you, but I am one of those people who is always curious about how things work. Recently, I was thinking about the old fashion (POTS) telephones. In case you don't know— or are too young— POTS stands for "Plain Old Telephone Service." POTS phones were connected by copper wires that you would then make phone calls from. You would often find these phones hanging on the wall in the kitchen, or sitting on the night stand next to the bed. They were notable by their long, flexible cords that reached out from the base. Many homes today still have the connection, although there is a major movement towards using cell phones instead. The interesting thing about those phones is that whenever there is a major power outage, those phones will more than likely to still work. So, of course, I wanted to understand why.

I've experienced situations where the power has gone out— not only in my immediate community, but also in the general area. My mobile phone occassionally worked, but that was not always a guarantee. It was always amazing that when all power went out,— including television, computers, cable, Internet, and everything else that required power— I could still make a phone call via a POTS phone if I needed. It seemed that throughout all of the problems and outages, I still had the opportunity to hear clearly what someone had to say to me via the telephone.

This situation is also very timely when we think about the way the Holy Spirit communicates. When I think about my life, I know for a fact that He is able to communicate with me no matter what is going on around me. It could be total silence caused by a power outage, or it could be total chaos and mayhem happening all around me; nevertheless, He is still able to speak directly to me. How does He do that? Let's explore this phenomenon in greater detail.

Most people never hear the Spirit of God communicating with them, nor do they perceive His voice. Why is that? The Bible explains this in several areas. Much like a radio needs an antenna in order to capture or receive the radio waves that are coming, we also have to have a way to receive and hear the Holy Spirit speaking. So what type of antenna should we have? Well, without going into too much detail, it essentially boils down to the fact that your spirit is intended to be the actual antenna to receive and hear what the Holy Spirit is saying.

When you look into the mirror, you see a reflection of who you are from an outward appearance. If you have brown hair, you will see the image of a person staring back at you with brown hair. If you have blue eyes, you will see the image of a person staring back at you with blue eyes. You see, in the mirror, the person that everyone else sees. It is your external— or fleshly— body. The Bible takes a different approach. The Bible teaches us that what we see in the mirror isn't all of who we are. Each of us is born with a spirit on the inside. We are also taught that we are made up of spirit, soul, and body. When we think about this, we realize that the saying is true that says, "There is more than meets the eye."

You may be thinking, "Great. Problem's solved. We have a spirit, and the Holy Spirit is a spirit; therefore we have the antenna we need." Unfortunately that is not the case. Until we have been born again through Jesus, our "antenna" is malfunctioning and is unable to receive what is being said. The Bible shares that due to sin and not knowing Jesus, our spirit is not alive; therefore, it is unable to recognize, perceive, and receive what the Holy Spirit is telling us. That's why the Bible stresses that we need to be born again. By receiving Jesus, our spirits are renewed and made alive. With a spirit that is now alive in us, we are able to receive, perceive, and hear what the Spirit of the Lord is telling us. This is why people who have yet to receive the Lord, have a difficult time believing and understanding the Holy Spirit.

Let's think about it in another way. Without an antenna, a radio cannot receive the radio waves. It doesn't even know that there are radio waves to receive; but once the antenna is installed, it hears and receives the messages. Your "antenna" must be installed in order for you to perceive and receive what the Holy Spirit is saying. When your antenna is alive, you have the ability to receive what is being downloaded to you, and you have the ability to communicate back. Communication with the Holy Spirit is not intended to be a one-way communication; instead, it is intended to be a conversation— which means you have the opportunity to respond. You are meant to be in constant dialogue: ask and answer.

One of the key things to remember when the Holy Spirit speaks, is that He speaks spirit to spirit. For lack of a better way of describing it, He often deposits His intentions into your spirit. He places a "deposit" directly to the inner you, the core of your being. For example, when someone types on a computer, the words that are typed come across the screen letter by letter. When the Holy Spirit places a deposit in your spirit, it is the entire sentence or thought all at once deposited on the inside of you; and He gives you just enough for you to be able to receive it. He knows not to give you too much at one moment, because you cannot process it. Instead, He gives you what you're able to digest. That's why I refer to it as a *deposit* that He places in you.

This deposit is more than a gut feeling. Gut feelings tend to be general feelings that often are void of clarity or specifics. When the Holy Spirit places a deposit inside of you (if you will listen intently), you will know it is from Him. He never directs you to do, or say anything, that is not aligned with the Bible. During the course of your conversation with Him, He provides clarity. The clarity that He gives provides direction, assurance, and the opportunity to change direction, if needed.

The speed in which His intent is downloaded into your spirit is amazing! It is as if the whole intent is downloaded to you in a blink of an eye. He does it in such a way that you know it came from Him and no one else. Even during the midst of a back and forth conversation, the answers can often come in that same manner such that you know what you're hearing; and even while you are asking a question, the response is coming back to you and being deposited. It is hard to find the precise words to describe the exact process by which this dowload works, but this is actually one method in which He does communicate.

As mentioned in the previous chapter, the Holy Spirit is a great teacher. He understands how much we can digest, and to that, I can attest. I remember early in my Christian walk— when I began to first hear the Holy Spirit communicating— I used to get frustrated. The information (or the revelation) I received from the Holy Spirit came in chunks, and I could not write them down fast enough. I was under the impression (and I have no idea why) that I needed to write syllable for syllable, and word for word, as He spoke. In actuality, He was giving me charts that I should be able to digest and remember. I eventually realized that there was no need to be frustrated. Instead, I would listen to what He said, and then capture in writing what I needed to absorb. From there, He would continue with the next thought, and my conversation with Him would finish out that part. I made sure to write down our conversation while it was still fresh in my memory; and I found that that method proved to be accurate, and less stressful.

Remember, when you build this communication with the Holy Spirit, and your spirit is alive, there is a confirmation of sorts inside of you that confirms who the originator of your message is. When it's the Holy Spirit, there is an affirmation or a confirmation inside of you that lets you know that it's Him. When it is the Holy Spirit speaking, it seems to permeate your whole being and deposits right into your very spirit. That message, then, seems to become a part of you. His communication to you seems like it "fits."

Alternatively, when you hear a conversation from

someone who is not the Holy Spirit, your spirit becomes agitated, and flags the message as something that you should stay away from. No matter how good the words might be, your spirit begins to let you know that it is not the voice of the Holy Spirit. You get this agitation, uneasiness, or the "something doesn't feel right" feeling that lets you know that it was not a word sent from the Holy Spirit.

One example of this happened to me many years ago when I was attending a Sunday morning church service. During that time, the church services would begin Sunday morning, but it wouldn't end until mid-afternoon. Some of you can relate to that! During one particular service, everyone who attended was earnestly engaged in the service: hands were clapping, voices were singing loudly, and the musicians were playing fabulously. Every word spoken before our guest speaker came to the podium was received well. The "amens" could be heard, and most people found it hard to sit due to the excitement. It was a lively service. When it was time for our guest speaker to minister, you could sense everyone's anticipation. He began with the traditional acknowledgment of the leaders, and welcoming everyone who was in attendance. From there, he began to preach his message. Not long into the message I began to feel a bit uncomfortable in my seat. It wasn't an alarm sounding inside of me or an agitation, but it seemed as though my "insides" were "leaping." As the message went deeper, it seemed as though the words the minister was preaching were aimed directly at me. Each word seemed to penetrate straight to my spirit. The funny thing was, he never looked at me. In fact, he did not even know me; but as he went deeper into his topic, it was as if the Holy Spirit was depositing straight into my spirit what I needed to hear. Now, I cannot attest to what the minister actually said, but I know the Holy Spirit was speaking directly into my spirit. It felt as though it fit directly, but I had never experienced that before. I first looked around to see if anyone else was experiencing what I was experiencing, but there was no indication that anyone else knew what I knew. By the time the message was completed, the Holy Spirit had confirmed and spoken to me in ways that I had never experienced, or understood, prior to that day. He spoke to me spirit to spirit.

The truth is, all of my life prior to that point, I had longed to hear the Spirit of the Lord speaking. Many folks that I had come across had talked about how the Holy Spirit spoke, but I had never personally experienced this for myself. From my perspective, it seemed like something wonderful. So, when I finally heard him speak to me, I was amazed! From there, I began to grow in ways that I could not have imagined prior to that point. The way that His words penetrated the walls and defenses I had built up, was amazing. Each word was targeted, and hit the direct points of my heart like none other. That Spirit to spirit communication was the beginning of my understanding of this relationship with the Holy Spirit. If you have not yet understood your relationship with Him, nor have you communicated with the Holy Spirit, I urge you to grow in that area.

As a Christian, we are all encouraged to read the Bible— the Old, as well as the New Testament— and I agree with that direction. The truth is, however, that it is sometimes difficult to understand the Bible during your early days as a Christian. Key points many "seasoned" Christians take for granted, are sometimes difficult to understand for new Christians. Fortunately, the Holy Spirit is there to help.

I love the account of Barnabas and Saul being sent out on a ministry assignment found in Acts 13.[22] In the first three verses, we see a lot about the Holy Spirit, and how He communicates. For instance, we see that several leaders of the local church had assembled to minister and to fast. Barnabas and Paul were among the group, since they had spent significant time helping the church to grow. They were seemingly accustomed to seeking the Lord together; and based on their titles, they had an established relationship with the Holy Spirit. My guess is as leaders of the church, they were seeking the Lord's direction for the church. With attentive hearts, they continued to pray and fast.

Finally, after a period of time, the Holy Spirit spoke. Now the Bible does not mention that the Holy Spirit spoke in an audible voice that everyone in Antioch could hear. In fact, the Bible just simply says, "the Holy Spirit said." Nothing more, nothing less. It is still very possible that He spoke audibly to all five leaders who were fasting and praying together. It is also very possible that He spoke directly to their spirits. What we do know is that they received the *same* message, because after fasting and praying, they sent Barnabas and Saul on their next mission, sanctioned by the Holy Spirit.

This account lets us realize that Spirit to spirit communication is not limited to just one-on-one conversation with the Holy Spirit. It is very possible, and likely, that He can deposit the same message simultaneously to multiple people. What He really looks for are those who are seeking direction; then He will provide it based on the will of the Lord. It is this wonderful download that occurs that allows you to know, without a doubt, that this is the Lord's will for your life. You will realize that the message just "fits." It is a perfect marriage of a hand in a glove; you just know that it's a confirmation to go ahead and take the next step.

I'm reminded of a situation a number of years ago where the wife of one of the deacons at my church had a stroke and became paralyzed. The stroke caused her to be confinced to a wheelchair. Upon learning the news, the church body proposed among ourselves to begin to intercede and pray for her healing. During that time period where the entire church body fasted and prayed, the men came together during a Men's meeting to spend time praying and interceding for her. We supported the husband (who was also there), and we began to pray in the spirit. The prayers were deep and and intense, and pulled from us greatly. We didn't let up until we felt an answer. I said "felt" because we didn't hear audibly like the leaders of the Antioch church heard, but we felt incensed that the answer was right there. We felt on that Saturday evening, that the Lord would do something major in our Sunday morning service. Again, I wanna stress that we didn't hear audibly, but we got this download in our spirits that gave us a confirmation that something would happen.

The next morning, during Sunday morning church service, the anticipation was high. Many of us had stayed on our fast, and were still looking and expecting the move of the Holy Spirit during the service. At the beginning of service, we saw the wife who had a stroke coming in via a wheelchair. As the service progressed, we got to the part of the praying and the laying of hands on the Deacon's wife. While this was happening, and the anticipation was palpable, with the whole church stretching their hands forward in faith believing that God is a true healer, the lady stood up and began to walk. You could hear the shouts of Hallelujah echoing throughout the whole church as if the roof was gonna fly off! As she walked, she began to praise God for herself; gradually regaining full movement and mental capacity. She moved forward and the church service left the pre-programmed service order in favor of giving God total praise and thanksgiving. The smiles, jubilation, and the looks of astonishment overwhelmed the whole sanctuary.

Fast forward to today, she is still healed, moving, and functioning fully. It was not a temporary thing. It was God's grace being poured out; and it was a confirmation to the download from the Holy Spirit speaking spirit to spirit amongst all of the local church. It was an affirmation of the confirmation that we had received. What a service that was!

*N*ow the Lord is the Spirit; and where the Spirit of the Lord is, there is liberty.

2 Corinthians 3:17

Was That You?

Chapter 6

How do you really know you if you are speaking to the Holy Spirit? Are you sure that what you heard was truly from Him, or was it your own desires? How can you tell the difference between when the Holy Spirit speaks, or something else? Was what you attribute as being the Holy Spirit really the result of watching news broadcasts all day? Or was it a prank played on you by a close friend or relative that used technology to make it seemed like you heard a voice? Or were you truly hoping and desiring a specific outcome in a situation, that it was your own hopes speaking, rather than the Holy Spirit? These are the types of questions and concerns that countless people wrestle with on a regular basis when trying to understand how the Holy Spirit speaks.

I enjoy discussing this topic. I have been to many small group meetings where this became a prominent topic. It always seemed to capture the curiosity and desire of those who were taking part in the discussions. Knowing what the Holy Spirit sounds like can be initially challenging to understand without direction. Fortunately, there are guidelines and examples listed in the Bible that are very helpful; however, it does take a desire to open the Bible and read, in order to find those answers. As I always say, "The Bible gives us answers to our questions; but we must have a desire to look for those answers."

To adequately begin this investigation, we should look at the verse mentioned at the beginning of this chapter. This is a short, but revealing part of scripture that helps us to understand the basis of who the Holy Spirit is, and how He speaks. This short verse shows us just how inseparable the Lord and his Spirit are. It shows that through the Spirit, we have liberty *and* freedom. That means freedom from everything that is causing bondage, depression, fear, lack, addiction, or anything that is not consistent with the Word of God. If we use that as our basis, then we understand that everything about the Holy Spirit is the same as the Lord's will. If we understand that, then we realize that conversations with Him will be about topics that cause freedom; and therefore, He points to the Kingdom of God. While pointing to the Kingdom of God, He's pointing to the King of kings— who is Jesus.

Have you ever met someone that always spoke about a particular topic in a particular way? You know the type that no matter what the conversation initially is, it always circles back to their favorite particular topic? Additionally, that person may have a mannerism, or a way in which they speak about that topic, that uniquely identifies that person.

For example, many young people today are wrapped up in video games. If you walk up to a 7 or 8-year-old and speak with them, oftentimes they want to tell you about their video games. If they have a favorite game, the conversation will always circle back to some aspect of that game. I've seen this happen repeatedly in my conversations with children that are 8 and under. It's fascinating and funny at the same time.

I had a cousin that was also this type of person. He was several years my elder, but he was born in the same town as me, and grew up around the same family members. Overall, he was a wonderful and caring man. Whenever he got together with the family, he would always talk about growing up as a country boy. He would mention the people, places, and activities he enjoyed as if it was paradise. The truth is, he grew up poor, but he really loved the simplicity of life during those times. As an adult, he often remembered the struggles he face; thus, he focused more on the simple things, and the love shared. His conversations always circled back to being a country boy, because that was the essence of how he considered himself.

In a similar manner, the essence of the Holy Spirit is one who brings freedom, joy, hope, laughter, good expectations, and much more. He cannot help but talk about the Lord and His purpose for each of our lives. Everything about Him aligns us with the will of the Lord. Since He is fervently focused on sharing the message of Jesus and His will for each of our lives, every aspect of the conversations with Him will reflect that purpose. So ask yourself, is what I am hearing in line with the Lord's will for my life? Does it reflect the Kingdom of God at all? If not, it is not the Holy Spirit speaking.

A great method to test the "voices" you are hearing is to read examples of when He's spoken in the past (via the Bible). Additionally, if you look at how Jesus described the Holy Spirit, you will understand what He will— and won't— say to you. For example, if you heard someone say, "Spend all your money, then ask God for more," that would not be the Holy Spirit. If you heard someone say, "Just curse at the person and tell them to get out of the way," that would also not be the Holy Spirit. Those two actions are contrary to what is written in the Bible. Therefore, you know that what you are hearing is not the Spirit of God.

I have been in ministry for many years, and I've heard many stories. What often simultaneously amazes and baffles me are the folks who say they are Christians, yet don't act like it at all. For instance, folks will always say, "I hear from God. I know what the Lord wants for me." However, they go and do things that are so obviously outside of the will of God, and then try to claim God did it.

I'll give you an easy example so as not to incriminate anyone. I knew a couple who were Christians, but were also caught up in their appearances and social status. They had a very nice house, and they always had new cars. They were successful, but I'm not sure where they were spiritually. On one Sunday morning, I saw the wife drive up to the church with a huge smile on her face. She had just purchased a brand new Porsche. Well, actually, she *leased* a brand new Porsche. The engine was revving as if it was eager to race, the body of the car glistened just right in the sunlight. She was professing to everyone that God had given her that Porsche, that the Lord had worked it all out. Everyone was amazed about what they thought God had done, based on what she had said. I'm telling you that that car was really nice!

However, there was a problem from my perspective. After she was telling everyone about what the Lord had done for her, she volunteered the information that kind of caught me by surprise: she confessed that her lease was over $1000 per month. That is a lot of money to pay for a lease. I was shocked, and I tried not to show my emotions or thoughts upon hearing that; since she was still so excited about what had happened. At that point I smiled, and I went back into the church building. On my walk back, I started thinking, "God that doesn't sound like you. Why would she get into a situation where it's $1,000 a month for at least three years, for a vehicle that she really didn't need, but she wanted to show?" This was just one thing, in a list of other not so great things, that I had been aware of about the couple that made this decision not add up at all. All of that to say, sometimes we convince ourselves that God is telling us something, but in reality, we're just acting upon our own impulses and desires.

If you are ever unsure about whether the Holy Spirit is guiding you, just remember what Jesus promised in John chapter 14:26:

*B*ut the helper the Holy Spirit whom the Father will send in *my name, he will teach you all things, and to bring to your remembrance all things that I said to you.*

That means the Holy Spirit has a purpose— or mandate— to continue to teach you if you will let him, and to bring back to your remembrance the word of God. If He's bringing back to your remembrance what Jesus said, then He surely is not telling you things that Jesus did not say. That is why it's important to understand what is in the Bible and what is not. With that being said, we must examine and be honest with ourselves about what we are experiencing and desiring.

As part of being in ministry, I have had numerous opportunities to counsel couples. Like most counselors, those couples have experienced varying results from the counseling. I've found that those who have listened to the advice that we have given, have turned out pretty well. The reason is, we spend time listening to what the Holy Spirit is saying about the couple and conveying the direction that the Holy Spirit wants them to take. So, in essence, I'm giving them the wisdom and advice that comes from the Bible, supported by the Holy Spirit. That advice is always designed to speak life into their relationship.

The key to any counselor, minister, or friend providing advice is to be sure your advice—wisdom— is coming from the Spirit of God. Otherwise, it is worthless. That is why it is imperative to have those around you who will provide truth, and not just tell you what you want to hear. You don't need someone else to tell you what you already want. A person is much more valuable to you if they provide you with truth and wisdom.

Let me wrap-up this chapter with the following thought. The Bible, especially in the New Testament, describes encounters with the Holy Spirit and the outcome of knowing Him. If you do your research, you will find the following words used:

1. Freedom
2. Liberty
3. Hope
4. Love
5. Joy
6. Peace
7. Longsuffering
8. Kindness
9. Goodness
10. Faithfulness
11. Gentleness
12. Self-control
13. Gift
14. Advocate

15. Teach
16. Speak
17. Power
18. Praying
19. Temple
20. Encourage

Although this is not an exhaustive list, these are words used extensively in association with the Holy Spirit. Now, ask yourself if what you are hearing— or feeling— falls into the categories these words represent? If everything you are hearing is leading you to be depressed, without hope, loveless, discouraged, and tumbling towards bondage, then it is not the Holy Spirit. Shut off everything that is not Him, and focus on the Good News— the Gospel. That's where you will find Him, and it will be the starting point of an everlasting relationship!

Now in the church that was at Antioch there were certain prophets and teachers: Barnabas, Simeon who was called Niger, Lucius of Cyrene, Manaen who had been brought up with Herod the tetrarch, and Saul. As they ministered to the Lord and fasted, the Holy Spirit said, "Now separate to Me Barnabas and Saul for the work to which I have called them." Then, having fasted and prayed, and laid hands on them, they sent them away.

Acts 13:1-3

The Order We Need

Chapter 7

Imagine if the Lord had given you—as you are now— the authority to plan the birth of the church (and everything that would happen afterwards), do you think you could do it? Obviously, the answer should be no. There are so many moving parts that impact other moving parts. How could you plan the order for the church to grow correctly? You would have to know every single moving part as it exists now, and in the future, in order for the growth to be successful. Your understanding would have to be beyond human comprehension. You would have to know where every person would be, at any given point in time, and the impact every single person would have on a family, a community, a town, a country, and the world. A vast amount of understanding would be necessary; and we all know that we don't possess that as human beings. That's why I am glad that I am who I am in Christ, and I don't have to worry about trying to be Him. What about you?

When I think about what happened at the church in Antioch,[23] I see some amazing things occurring. Not only did the Holy Spirit speak, He put things in order. Before I tell you what I am referencing, I would encourage you to reread those verses at the beginning of this chapter. As the verses clearly state, the prophets and teachers of the church in Antioch gathered together to minister to the Lord. That means, they were seeking guidance and direction from Him. They made it their sole focus to find out what the Lord would have them to do next. We should be of that same mindset, and take out time in our daily lives to seek the Lord in order to understand what He wants us to do each and every day.

While they were seeking the Lord, the Holy Spirit began to speak to them. In the scripture it doesn't specifically say the method in which He spoke, but it could have been audibly or it could have been Spirit to spirit; and the Bible never alludes to anyone outside of that group hearing the Holy Spirit speak. I don't know about you, but I've heard of circumstances (and I have experienced instances) where the Holy Spirit speaks in the midst of a group of folks, but only certain people there. Just like after Jesus was baptized, God spoke— but only some understood what He said. A few perceived this same event as thunder, while others weren't even sure that there was a noise or a voice. A phenomena like that can happen when the Holy Spirit speaks. Remember, your antenna is there to receive what the Holy Spirit is saying.

What we do know, is that the Holy Spirit spoke the same message to all of them. He gave them direction as to what was needed for the next phase of the ministry. In other words, what the Lord wanted to happen next, is what the Holy Spirit was revealing. The ones that were seeking the Lord were wise, because they did not assume they knew the perfect next step; but, instead, they realized that they needed to ask the Lord. The Holy Spirit, then, took charge and began to distribute the available resources. In this case, Barnabas and Saul were the resources— or tools— that needed to be deployed. The Bible never says that other resources were not used; it just so happens the account follows Barnabas and Saul.

The Spirit of God, who is omniscient, understood that the church needed to expand. He understood that there were fertile hearts to the west of Antioch. He also understood that the vessels that He had been preparing, were now ready. Therefore He sent Barnabas and Saul on the missionary journey. He was able to see the timing *and* the need *and* the qualified resources, in order to bring about the results that He knew He wanted.

Although no one knows for sure, the prophets and teachers may have just been seeking guidance regarding issues within their local church; however, the Holy Spirit gave direction that would affect the global church. We often address and pray for things we are locally experiencing, whereas the Holy Spirit addresses the local *and* global church. He knows which resources to use for every assignment.

When the Holy Spirit works with us, He utilizes what's in us (even as we are developing more in Him) at the proper time period, because he is able to understand all of the moving parts; all of the emotions that are erupting; all of the current needs; and the strategy needed to accomplish the task. He is more than capable of putting plans in order for a successful life, journey, and expansion of the Kingdom. If we take a step back for a minute, and look at how the Holy Spirit works, the level of perfection and timeliness that He displays should amaze us. Knowing this, it is also amazing that we, as people, continue to have issues with trusting Him. His record is flawless, while ours is flawed. We all should run to Him, lettting Him plan everything; but there is something inside of us that does not want to let go of control. We should all strive to overcome that through the grace of the Lord.

Placing things in their proper order is something the Holy Spirit does really well. This applies to business dealings, relationships, and in every other aspect of your life. One key area within a relationship where this really applies, is a marriage. No matter how good and sound your marriage is, there are points in that marriage where it gets challenging. There are moments where disagreements can arise. When you have a couple that has a relationship with the Lord, and listens to the Holy Spirit's guidance, you have a great way to resolve conflicts. In a Godly marriage, what often happens— and I've heard it said to me on multiple occasions— is when a couple is at a point of disagreement, they yield to see what the Lord would say about the issue. As time progresses, the Holy Spirit begins to address the issue: Spirit to spirit. If one member of the marriage couple is totally in the wrong, the Holy Spirit will speak to them, and, in many cases, that person will acknowledge their misstep and apologize. Oftentimes, there are shortcomings on behalf of both members of the couple. The Holy Spirit will speak to both of them, in order to help them come to a resolution. Some people will have trouble believing that He is that engaged in a couple's relationship, but it is true. When both members of a marriage value and listen to the Holy Spirit's direction, there is less friction and more resolution.

When you commit yourself to the Lord and want to follow Him, what you are inferring is that you are willing to let Him lead your life in order for your life to be all that He designed it to be. That means every aspect of your life is supposed to be surrendered to Him. Does that mean we're perfect from the start? Of course not! What actually happens, is we gradually release portions of our life to the Holy Spirit, while still desperately holding on to other portions. Since we gradually release only parts of our life, it takes longer for us to see the full effect of the Lord in our life. It can be frustrating, but oftentimes we are the source of the frustration. Think about that for just a moment.

Now let me stop at this point in the chapter to explain something that may be confusing to you. We can agree that God has given all of us capabilities and talents. Since He's given us these gifts and talents, He expects us to use those talents for the good, and His glory. What about when it comes to decision-making? We know that when it comes to making decisions, there are some things that you do, and some things that you don't have to stop and pray for an hour to get an answer about. Right? For instance, if your trash can is running over in the kitchen, do you think you need to stop and pray in order to see whether or not you should empty the trash? I would think the answer is, no. If your roof is leaking, do you think you need to wait and pray to see whether or not you should do something about it? I would think the answer is no, still. You may pray about which contractor to choose, but if you learn to trust in the Lord— and have a relationship with Him— you already know the answer based on what is given to you. In essence, there are some general things that we are able to just "know." However, there are many other things that we should at least ask in prayer about whether they are the right things to do, or not. On one spectrum, there are people who never know to ask or pray about anything; on the other end of the spectrum, there are those who pray about things that they can just take care of themselves. Hopefully, after reading this book, you will be able to know the difference between the two; and, be able to live life fully while maintaining a strong relationship with the Lord.

Throughout my career, I've often emphasized the importance of timeliness. I am not restricting it to just arriving to meetings on time, but I'm focusing more on understanding the time and the season in which the Lord is operating. Some of the things that He would have us to do early in our Christian walk, is very different from what He would have us to do later. Timeliness is very important to the Holy Spirit. More grace is given early in your relationship with Him, than later. Understanding when to act upon the Holy Spirit's direction is crucial. The moment when God is moving, is when we should be in that same flow and moving also. I've shared frequently that even though you may have a good word to share, or a desire to generously give to help someone, it may not be adequate or appropriate in the current time. That's why we must constantly be aware of how the Holy Spirit is moving.

For example, I have known several great guys who know they were called by the Lord for a specific purpose in the church; many put off the call because they wanted to deal with "life" first. In several of those cases, many years have passed. Now, their opportunities to serve in the areas they were called to have dried up, or have dramatically diminished. What they did not take into account was the timing of the Lord's call. If they had responded positively to the call when it was issued, all the necessary resources to ensure success would already be aligned for them. The Holy Spirit would arrange everything for them in a way that would ensure success. Unfortunately, they did not understand the importance of timeliness.

I urge you to consider the examples that I outlined in this chapter. All of them are there to provide clarity, and hopefully, an incentive for you to let the Holy Spirit guide and arrange your next steps. Just think for a minute, if Saul or Barnabas were not in their place when the Holy Spirit was ready to Commission them for their mission, what would have happened? Would they have missed their opportunity to serve? Would they have missed their blessing? Would they have missed a great opportunity to grow? The answer is, probably yes. There are many of us who miss our calling on a daily basis by not being aware of the season and the times. Additionally, we miss it because we have this issue of letting go, and letting God. The Holy Spirit will arrange everything, so we must trust that He's got it under control. He is expressly doing the will of the Lord in your life; which means that everything is already arranged. Just trust and go.

Now hope does not disappoint, because the love of God has been poured out in our hearts by the Holy Spirit who was given to us.

Romans 5:5

Gentle and Loving

Chapter 8

What does the Holy Spirit sound like? How often does He speak? What types of conversations does He partake in? These, and countless other questions, are usually brought up when discussing the Holy Spirit. You see, I realize this concept, and the understanding of this Person called, the Spirit of God, is something that people don't normally hear about, nor do they all understand it; but the Holy Spirit is discussed throughout the Bible from the beginning to the end. Knowing this, through deeper reading and understanding, you begin to realize that He interacts with us, and is a person that is with us, on a daily basis.

So what type of personality does He possess? That's a good question. Hopefully, the title of this chapter will give you some understanding of what I found to be His character; however, we're still going to spend some time discussing it in more detail. The purpose of writing this entire book was to give you a good understanding of who the Holy Spirit is and what He is like. In order to do that, I've been flooding you with an array of examples so you can grasp the interactions that, you too, can have with him. He didn't set things up to only talk to one person. Anyone who is born again has the privilege of being able to build that relationship with Him.

If I had to describe His personality, I would definitely say that he is gentle and loving. He is one that is always there, and is eager to have more interactions with us; but He will wait for us to allow Him into our lives. The Holy Spirit is the manifestation of the power of God, but yet still, He wants us to welcome a relationship with Him, as opposed to forcing the interaction. Since He won't force a relationship— and this is based on my own personal experiences— I would describe Him as gentle. Additionally, I would say that He's loving. With every interaction with the Holy Spirit, you can feel the love by the way He speaks; and you can tell in every interaction that He cares for our well being. Jesus even spoke about the reason He came— to give us life, and life more abundantly.[24] One of the ways in which this is realized is through the gift of the Holy Spirit, and his continual presence.

Let me take a moment to illustrate a couple of examples that will hopefully help you picture and grasp what I'm sharing with you. Years ago, before I was even married, I was coming back from hanging out with some friends at the University of Maryland. For those who are familiar with this area, you know the University of Maryland is located just inside of the Capital Beltway; and the Capitol Beltway circles Washington. D.C. In contrast, Baltimore, also has a beltway that circles the city; and Interstate 95 (I-95) connects them.

On that particular night, I left College Park MD and drove up I-95 towards Baltimore. Of course, I was hanging out later than I should have, but I was determined to get home. As I was "flying" up 95 at speeds that I will not disclose, I became sleepy a little more than halfway up the Interstate. As much as I tried to stay awake— winding the windows down, turning the radio up, shifting in the seat— I eventually fell asleep at the wheel. However, I didn't realize it. Before I knew it, I was starting to careen to the middle, grassy area that separates the North and Southbound traffic. Although it was a wide, grassy area, it formed a steep decline that ended in a ditch. If I had hit that area at the speed in which I was traveling, I would not be here to write this book.

What I do remember during that brief moment that I was asleep, was a loud voice shouting, "JAMES!" My eyes snapped open, and I saw myself headed for disaster. There was no one physically in the car with me, nor was there someone speaking through a phone or anything else. I saw the impending crash coming, and I aggressively turned the wheel just in time to avoid a terrible accident. Once I gained control of the vehicle, I got out of the fast lane, and drove at the posted speed. My heart was pounding, and I was trying to regain my composure. I knew without a doubt that it was the Holy Spirit that woke me up.

Although the voice was a shout in order to get my attention, I also knew that it was a shout of love. He saw the accident that was about to happen, and He intervened to make sure that it did not occur. It reminded me of a parent who, out of concern for their child, shouts aggressively to get the child's attention— especially if the child is near something, or someone, dangerous. They may yell or shout at the child, but it is for the child's safety that they do it. I felt the same way in that moment, because if the Holy Spirit had not called my name, I wouldn't be here to write about.

Let me give you yet another example. Have you ever been in a situation where your anxiety is high, and you feel as though you do not have clarity of thought because there's so much running through your mind? Have you been in a situation where you are pressured to make a quick decision? In addition to that, have you felt the need to make a right decision for the sake of others? If so, those are recipes for a very stressful situation. It is well documented in business— and just human nature— that making decisions under duress or stress may cause you to make the wrong decision; in contrast, it's easy to think about what a person should do when you are not the one in the situation. I remember a number of situations where I felt like I had to make a major decision, but I didn't feel like I had all of the right information. Additionally, it felt as though time was ticking as if there was a clock in my ear. In those times, I remember asking on multiple occasions, "Where are you?" Of course I was asking the Holy Spirit, since in those cases, it seemed like He was so quiet. As I was searching to hear His voice, it felt like I heard nothing. So what was I to do? I had to make a decision, right?

After diligently searching for an answer, and getting closer to the decision deadline, I finally got an answer. The Holy Spirit simply and gently said, "I'm here." His response was so easy; I couldn't help but wonder why such a simple response took so long. However, as it turned out, His guidance came just in time, which caused the decision I made to be the correct decision. It was almost as if He was testing me, to see if I would lose faith and try to just do it on my own; or if I would patiently wait for His answer. Sure, He gives us wisdom and understanding, but we also should put our plans in front of the Lord for approval. That process of putting the plans in front of Him for approval can be challenging. If you are anything like me, I like to get things done in a timely manner. Those who know me will even acknowledge that I do not like being late. That's a great trait to have, except when you are waiting for an answer. Then it is no longer something within my control! Jesus, however, is always on time, and He'll deliver— through the Holy Spirit— the right answer. So we have to learn to wait and listen, so we can make right decisions.

The Holy Spirit's gentleness is remarkable. There are many times that I am agitated, impatient, and even anxious to get things done, but His gentleness calms me down. What I have found out in countless situations, is that my desire to quickly get things done is not always the best approach. In every case where He's got me to tone down my impatience, I have discovered that there were variables that I did not see, recognize, or understand; and these variables would have caused me more pain, anguish, frustration, or harm. But He did— He knew it all before it ever occured. That is why I am slowly getting better and better at listening and waiting for direction.

Since the Holy Spirit knows each of so well, I can attest that His personality— and the way that He personally interacts with me— is perfect! I am certain that He looks at our individual personalities and understands how to best get points across to each of us. You may be the polar opposite of me, in that you procrastinate frequently, and He has to get you to respond quicker. What method He uses to get the results necessary, is up to Him. Just remember, He does this for your good, and for the good of the Kingdom of God.

Did you expect me to say that He is one who just commands you to do things, and that was it? Did you expect the Holy Spirit to be very impersonal, as opposed to personal? Have you ever given thought to what He is like? Again, I stress that He is definitely gentle and loving. All throughout the Bible— from beginning to end— it speaks about how much God loves us (there is no difference in this relationship because we are the temple). So always remember, regardless of what's going on in your life, He is there to help you, and to guide you, if you allow Him. As I mentioned in a previous chapter, you will always know when it's the Holy Spirit, because He will never contradict the Word of God. He will never ask you to do things that are contrary to the teachings of Jesus. He will never force you, or encourage you, to do something that is harmful to you. He is One who cares about your well being.

In your relationship with Him, you can still be a confident person (not to be confused with arrogance or pride), but make sure that your confidence is based on Him and your relationship with Him. Make sure that as you walk in confidence, that it is based on experience (with the Holy Spirit); make sure your confidence comes from knowing that you're on the right path because you know that He will come through. As I mentioned before, I have deliberately opened myself to listen for what the Holy Spirit is directing me to do. There are a number of times that I've gotten it wrong due to impatience, a desire not to hear what is being said, or not listening at all; but it is so sweet when you do take the time to listen. Listening and aligning yourself with what He tells you to do is where we experience the results.

A number of years ago, I was working for a multi-billion dollar corporation. I had been there for a number of years, but I was starting to feel that it was time to transition to a different company. The current organization was a wonderful place to work, but it was also going through its own major transitions. At this job, the Lord had elevated me into a number of wonderful positions that allowed me to experience things that I only dreamed of. As the feeling of transition began to grow within me, I had no idea what company, or organization that I should go and work for; but without a doubt, inside of me, I knew that the time was coming where I needed to leave. So, I began to pray and ask the Holy Spirit for direction. For a while it was quiet, and I got no response. However, I kept listening and asking, in hopes that something would be said. Unfortunately, it was totally silent. He was not saying anything that I could hear at that time, *but* I learned to trust Him because He had been so faithful over the years prior. As the days went on, I knew without a doubt that it was getting close to time to transfer to a different company. Then one day, another Christian who worked with me, explained to me that during their prayer time with the Lord, that He told them that it was time for me to move on from the company. This time, fortunately, there were more specifics that this person gave me. I had not given them all the details prior to my conversation with them, so I knew it had to be from the Holy Spirit. I also knew because my internal spirit was agreeing, and it felt like this was really the Holy Spirit speaking to me. In addition to that person, there was yet another person who called, and told me the Holy Spirit revealed to her that I needed to be moving to a another organization. Prior to her sharing that with me, I had not given her the details of what was happening. In all of this, you see, the Holy Spirit was speaking, but based on His wisdom, He was communicating through others directly to me.

What this entire situation did was confirm to me that He was actively involved in moving me to where I needed to go. Just like I mentioned in another chapter, the Holy Spirit understands who is born again, and He is familiar with all of their capabilities— even if they aren't familiar with their own capabilities. He deploys and moves people, as needed, for the benefit of the glory of God, through the Kingdom of God. He knows the right timing and the correct situations in which our skills and abilities will go the farthest. In that situation, He let me know in advance, that the move was coming; and He confirmed it by others, before it finally happened.

Since I am a temple of the Holy Spirit, He has to let me

know where we are going. My job is just to *listen*. Everything worked exactly as He had placed in my spirit (and as others had confirmed). It's amazing how precise and timely He is. One key thing I remember clearly is, during that time, preparing to move from one company to another, He was so caring that He guided me step by step. Like some human beings, I don't mind change, but I approach it cautiously. He knew that, so it was almost like He was taking me by the hand, walking with me every step of the way. He walked me through identifying the right timing; He walked me through the interview process, and highlighted things that I should be aware of; He walked me through the process of deciding where I should work, or whose offer I should accept. Additionally, He worked out the salary and the time frame in which all of this should happen. It was just amazing! I'm excited even as I write this because I remember, with fondness, how deeply involved He was. However, I also realize that some of you would say that you've never experienced that level of involvement from the Holy Spirit. Don't worry! If you are born again,[25] and you are interested in growing your relationship with the Holy Spirit— who is the gift from God— then open your heart[26] and begin to work on your relationship with Him.

Still supporting the point that I made about the Holy Spirit being loving and gentle, there is an amazing verse in the Bible that can be found in Ephesians 4:30. In it there is a directive from the apostle Paul that says, "and do not grieve the Holy Spirit of God, with whom you were sealed for the day of redemption." He uses the word grieve as if sorrow can be associated with the Holy Spirit. If He can experience sorrow (or grief) that not only proves that He is a person, but that He cares. It proves that when things are not the way they should be, it causes sadness or sorrow. That means He cares about how we live, and how we interact with Him. It's amazing that the Spirit of God, who is first revealed in the book of Genesis, cares about our lives to the extent that He can be grieved. As I told you before, He is gentle and loving, and He wants to build a relationship with you in order for you to understand His role and His purpose in the Kingdom of God. It's a wonderful and special privilege that all of us have who have been born again, have. Just pause for a minute. Imagine that you are standing on a mountaintop. What do you see around you? Do you see a continuous mountain vista in the distance? Does snow cover the peaks? Is the air crisp and clean? Do you see town lights in the distance? Really imagine it. Can you imagine being surrounded by such immense beauty! Now, can you image how many people may exist within that town in the distance? A few dozen? A few hundred? Thousands? How many are adults? Elderly? Children? Each and every person has their own wants, desires, and aspirations; and they're not always happy. Can you manage them? Thankfully, we don't have to. It's even better with the Holy Spirit, because as One who is eternal, and cares about each one of us even though we don't do everything we say we should do, He's still there. Amazing!

*O*r do you not know that your body is the temple of the Holy Spirit who is in you, whom you have from God, and you are not your own? For you were bought at a price; therefore glorify God in your body and in your spirit, which are God's.

1 Corinthians 6:19-20

His Temple

Chapter 9

This verse has always intrigued me. It boldly states that we are a temple.[27] A Temple? How can we be a temple? When I think of temples, I think of the large buildings from ancient times devoted to various gods. I think of large pillars that are set up, supporting these very large edifices. I think of buildings that are on a high mountain, that take a long journey in order reach it. Additionally, from a Biblical perspective, I think of the Tabernacle that the children of Israel had. I also think of the temple that Solomon built, and the temple that Herod built. Now, when I think about those temples, I have a hard time comparing it to the temple that Paul was speaking of.

So, in order to get a grasp of this concept of a temple, I had to do what all people do when they're trying to understand. They look in the dictionary (and any other supporting materials). As I looked at various definitions, I began to gravitate to a definition of a temple that connects most of the other individual definitions. So what I found out, in a general sense, is a temple is a place where God dwells. It is also a place of service and worship to God. So a temple by definition— or be it my definition— is a place that is in the presence of God. It isn't one of the archaeological finds that visitors from all over the world go and see. In those cases, they are intriguing and interesting, but God doesn't dwell there. The temple that Paul is referencing is a little bit different.

If God dwells in this temple, then this temple must be special. If God dwells in this temple, then this temple must experience supernatural phenomena on a regular basis. If God dwells in this temple, there must be constant interaction and communication with Him. When I look at the temple from that perspective, that gives me an understanding of how our lives should be. Think about it for a minute. If we are a temple, then we must have some relationship to God. In our case, our relationship to God is through the Holy Spirit. If we are the temple, then we must know Him and have some type of relationship with Him. So what is He like? What things does He say? We should be able to answer those questions.

I count it a privilege to know that the Holy Spirit dwells in me (and others) who have received Christ. That means that *all* things are now possible. One of those things is to be able to communicate and speak with the Holy Spirit on a regular basis. We do not have to limit our conversations with Him, either, since He's been in existence before time ever existed. He is the Spirit of God, therefore He knows and sees everything. So what kind of questions could we ask, or what types of conversations could we have with Someone who has seen everything and knows everything to come? Well, the answer is endless conversations. That's what He truly desires.

Do you have someone that you would consider your best friend? Maybe you have more than one, but I would guess that you really have less than five. For those people who have best friends, there are conversations that you can have with them, that you can't have with anyone else. In fact, you have conversations that are never ending it seems. You probably have a friend that you've known even from decades ago, yet you still feel comfortable in their presence; and you can strike up a conversation without much effort. With your friend, you can talk about any topic and not feel as though you have to be guarded. You can also listen to your friend's feedback, because you trust them. Our relationship with the Holy Spirit should be even closer than that.

Since I am a temple of the Holy Spirit, and Jesus said the Holy Spirit would teach us all things, I have put forth a direct effort to develop my conversation and communication with Him. My conversations are not limited— at all— because I want to get the truth and the right answers. I think it's silly to try to hide aspects of your life from the Holy Spirit because He knows it all anyway. Therefore, I ask and confess everything. I confess and talk about relationships, finances, emotions, career, the future, meanings of Bible verses, and much more. I will even share things that I think are funny that someone has said. Now before we go any further, I don't want you to think that I walked down the street looking up at the sky talking into thin air as I walk down crowded streets. That's not how it works (although there may be situations where you may utter a question or a phrase). Most of my communication when I'm in public doesn't require me to start talking out loud to make a spectacle of myself. I am a temple, therefore I can speak internally to Him, and we can have a conversation.

As I have deliberately developed my relationship with the Holy Spirit, I have found myself asking for direction and clarification on *all* of life's issues that come my way. As you may recall from my story in an earlier chapter, when I was managing a large team for a private company, there was a major deliverables issue that arose. As that issue developed, I found myself wondering what was happening. I asked the Holy Spirit what I needed to do to fix the situation, and how I needed to proceed. In essence, I was asking for clarification of the origin of the issue, and a plan to rectify and fix the situation. Believe it or not, He began to lay the issue out in front of me, the cause of the problem, and the solution. He laid out the plan, then I took it and began to apply it to the situation. Of course, the plan was successful. To be truthful, every time that I've actually listened to His direction, everything has worked out marvelously. The problem is, I don't always listen as intently as I should. I am working on improving in that area; and I'm sure that I am not the only one!

As I mentioned in another chapter, the Holy Spirit knows how to communicate to each one of us. He knows how to get His point across in a way that we can understand. So how does He do that? Well, since we are the temple, and He dwells in His temple, then He knows us well and He interacts with us regularly even when we don't acknowledge it. He understands our personalities and our trigger points. Because of that, He is able to craft messages that will be received by us so that we can be successful in every endeavor. The great thing about being the temple of the Holy Spirit is that wherever you go, He is with you. You could be on the other side of the world far from your home, but He is still there. You could be at the North Pole by yourself, but He is still there. You understand my point?

I've even asked the Holy Spirit for directions— more frequently than I would care to admit. I know, this may seem silly and trivial, but it is actually true. Although I have my own GPS (via the phone and oftentimes in the vehicles) that I'm driving, sometimes I really need to rely on His GPS to get me to the intended place at the right time. As you should be used to by now, I have an example. Years ago, I was searching for a church home. Sure, my family and I had relocated to a new area, but what was really driving this search was this insatiable hunger for more of God. The places where I had attended were great, but I needed a deeper encounter and understanding of His word. My wife and I spent over a year traveling from church to church each Sunday, in order to see which one was the one where the Lord would want us to attend. On one of these Sunday mornings, we got up and started driving. We had no particular church in mind, but we knew we had to keep looking. So, we started driving and making turns— left and right— but not really knowing where our destination was. On those types of journeys, a physical GPS in your phone or in your car cannot help you. You are looking for the God Positioning System (GPS) to direct you to where you need to go. In other words, it is the Holy Spirit guiding you. As we made a series of turns in areas that I had not been previously, I could hear at every intersection the Holy Spirit saying, "Turn here." Finally, I came to a road with a sign that read 'dead end.'

I had a choice, then. I could keep going— even though the road was a dead end— or I could turn around and head in another direction. Even though the sign said the road was a dead end, we still drove down the road. Lo and behold, there was a church at the end of the road. We didn't know that when we turned onto the street, but sure enough there was a church. We were early, and people were literally just starting to pull into the parking lot. I asked one of the deacons for more information about the church, and afterwards we decided that we would set aside time to visit the following week. We did visit the church the following week— and several weeks afterwards— until the Lord told us this was where we needed to be. The God Positioning System never fails.

I have utilized the God Positioning System on countless occasions. Because I know that He abides in this temple, and I acknowledge His authority, I can see Him work. Therefore, I know that He travels with me, so I'm always able to get direction. That direction could result in a destination, but it also takes into account the timing of arrival. The everyday Global Positioning System that we used in our phones and in our vehicles, often gives you an estimated time of arrival based on what it knows about the traffic volume, the number of traffic lights, and the speed limit. To an even a greater degree, the God Positioning System allows us to roughly know the timing of arrival based on His desire and His expectation. We can know this when we develop a relationship with Him, since we are the temple and He abides in that temple. I would encourage you to realize that the Holy Spirit is in you, if you are born again. It's a simple thing to do, but people make it so complicated because it seems so different. In my case, I am one of those people who will read the Bible, and then believe what it says. That makes everything easy.

When you think about temples, regardless of the religion, they all seem to have places to store sacred writings. These writings are usually available to the priest, and leaders to come and read and to meditate upon. These writings usually give instruction about life, and how it should be lived. The same is true when it comes to the Tabernacle that Moses erected. In the

Holy of holies was the very presence of God; but inside the ark in the holy of holies, is also the Commandments. These writings that the Jewish people were commanded to live by, were in this Tabernacle. Knowing this, we must ask ourselves a simple question. What writings have to be in us if we are the temple? Well the answer is pretty obvious, I believe. The writings need to be scriptures from the Bible, that we have read and committed to memory *and* committed to our life. The more of the writings— or the word of God— that abide in us, in the temple, the more revelation of the Spirit of God and the will of the Lord is seen in us. We must have the word of God abiding in this temple. That tells us that if we want this temple to be full of God's glory, we must have more of His word inside of us.

When I was a child, my family attended a community church up the street from our home. In that church, there was a large Bible that always stayed on one of the podiums. You know the types that are extremely large in size, and very large print? A guest, or a minister, or lay leader,[28] would read certain scriptures from that Bible based on what's written in the bulletin. Additionally, there would often be extra Bibles on the seats for those that came in to read. This was a way for the sacred writings to be available in the temple. In today's society, many people bring their Bible on their phones, tablets, or other electronic devices. You don't often see physical Bibles in the chairs and pews, to the extent we used to. Even so, we are still adhering to the understanding that sacred writings have to be in the temple.

When was the last time you tried to memorize a Bible verse? When was the last time you read, and meditated on, the promises of Lord? Has any of that sunk into you such that you can utilize it at any time? Does the temple have the word available? This is important because the Holy Spirit may address situations that arise in your life with scripture. For example, earlier this year, I found myself hospitalized. What continued to rise up in my spirit was a Bible verse: Proverbs 18:14. The verse reminds me that "a strong spirit of a man shall sustain him." I looked at this as a message directly from the Holy Spirit, since I am the temple. It was reminding me that the Lord had everything in control. As I meditated on that, other scriptures began rising up inside of me. These verses were things that I had memorized years ago— but put together, they were telling a story of what the Lord was doing (and providing reassurance about my situation at that time). All throughout my hospital stay this continued to occur. It was a conversation between the Holy Spirit and I. In fact, I focused so much on continuing that conversation, that I tuned out the calls and expressions of concern from friends and loved ones. You see, at that moment, there was only one Person who could help me. So, I focused on Him.

By giving you this example, I am hoping that you begin to consider how important it is to hear what the Spirit of the Lord is saying. Think about it for a minute, and realize that the Spirit of God knows the heart of God. You are hearing exactly what God wants you to know, because the Holy Spirit is God. If you are then able to receive what's being said, you can have direction and communication no matter where you are on the face of the earth, and no matter what situation you face today. This is something that can only come from God. The Bible describes the Holy Spirit as a gift. A gift is something that the giver hopes, and is pretty confident, that you will like and enjoy. Additionally, a gift is something that you may need; therefore, the giver is expressing his love toward the one who receives the gift. Thus, in the gift of the Holy Spirit, we have a great expression of love.

You might ask yourself why you are not having the level of interactions with the Holy Spirit that I am referencing. Just know that if you are a born again Christian, you have to nurture and develop that relationship. When a person goes into ministry for the first time, there are many hurdles and unknowns that the new minister will face. It takes time to learn everything, and to interact at every level that is required. If a new minister quit on the first day, that minister will never able to properly minister in the way that he was intended. However, if he continues to learn, develop, and practice his calling, he will have more and more revelation, interaction, and deliverance manifested in his ministry. Likewise, as the temple of God, the more you nurture and practice that relationship, the more it develops and manifests in every aspect of your life. Do you want to grow and know the Holy Spirit even more? It really is up to you. Just know that if you are hungry for more, you will begin to experience more of the Spirit of God.

Did you know that there are people who spend all of their waking hours at a temple? This is true no matter what the religion is. You can always find examples of this throughout the world. In the Bible, there was an account of a widow who spent all of her years of widowhood at the temple that Herod built. Through all of those hours and years that the widow spent at the temple, she got to know the Holy Spirit very intimately. One day, when Jesus was brought to the temple, she prophesied about His life. She was only able to do that because of the relationship that she developed with the Lord all those years in the temple.

When you spend that much time, and commit that level of focus, you get to know the One who you are spending time with. Just like married couples who have been married for decades seem to finish each other sentences, and know what's on each other's mind without ever verbally expressing it, it is the same with the amount of time you spend with the Holy Spirit. As the temple, when you take advantage of the time that's available for you to spend with Him, you will get to understand Him more than someone who does not spend much time with Him. You will begin to understand His personality, the things that drive Him, the things that He does not like, and His purposes. The more time you spend with Him, the more your heart is aligned with His. In essence, you become one.

Take time to remember, respect, and nurture the special relationship that you have as the temple. This is something that is uniquely given to each born again believer. It is a gift, therefore, we need to cherish that gift. I encourage you, as I've done in other chapters, to nourish that relationship by putting it first. Began to seek the will of the Lord through the Holy Spirit. He abides in you, so acknowledge who He is, and your relationship with Him.

Pilate said to Him, "What is truth?"

John 18:38

Worship In Spirit and Truth

Chapter 10

What is truth? Generations upon generations of people have sought to understand this question. Pilate[29] asked that very question of Jesus. Even Pilate, although considered learned, didn't understand what Jesus was saying, nor did he understand the truth. The struggle to identify what truth really means has hounded every generation. Many of you have heard— and perhaps use— the phrase 'define your truth.' It's also formatted as 'live your truth.' Yet, even with those sayings that try to define and grasp the realities that people live in, there still is no understanding of the truth: a universal one. Jesus came in order to tell us what truth meant, but the majority of the people still didn't (and still don't) understand. So, let's examine the truth; let's also ask ourselves the question, 'What does the truth have to do with the Holy Spirit speaking?'

From our natural perspective, truth deals with things that are experienced, or known to be. It may be truthful that the sky is blue, or that the sky can sometimes be gray. We know this because we see it and observe it on a regular basis. Therefore, it seems to be true, right? What about those things that we only see in part? Are they true? Centuries ago, people thought the world was flat. They came to that conclusion simply from looking at the horizon. It *seemed* flat. The horizon looked as though everything would go to a certain point, then fall off. To them, the truth was, the world was flat. During that time when they lived with that 'truth,' the *real* truth told a different story. The real truth: the world is round. Once they came to that understanding, their truth changed. For us to understand the purpose of the Holy Spirit and how He speaks, we have to deal with the real truth.

Jesus is described in the Bible on a number of occasions as being the Truth. That means, He is the essence of all truth; and everything that comes through Him, and out of Him, is true. With that basic understanding, we can infer that ***everything Jesus taught is based on truth, and is truth***. It is based on how things truly are, as opposed to how we perceive them to be. It is in this same space that the Holy Spirit operates. If you recall, earlier in this book I told you that the Holy Spirit had several jobs; one of those jobs is to point to everything that Jesus taught during His ministry. If He's pointing to what Jesus taught, that means He's pointing to the truth. However, He not only points us to the truth, one of His jobs is to continually *remind* us of the truth. That happens to be one of the key reasons why He is here; He realises that the more of the truth that we know, the more our lives will change for the better.

When I was a child, based on the things that I had heard and seen, I thought being a Christian meant being a good person and going to church. I thought that that was all there was to it; and I didn't yet realize the truth. It took a while for me to understand that I could never earn my salvation; that it was solely through grace that I had been saved. It also took a while for me to understand that Jesus made me a new creation once I got saved. So, how did I finally understand that truth? The Holy Spirit taught me. At the time, I didn't know what to call Him, but my understanding began to increase the more that I thought and meditated on what the process of being a Christian meant, and how that process happened. The Holy Spirit was little by little giving me more of an understanding, and working in my heart to draw me to the call of the Lord. At that time, I only recognized Him by the functions he fulfilled, and the pulling inside of me.

That was the extent of the communication that I had. It was the only communication I was mature enough to handle.

When it came time for me to truly understand the truth— and I was mature enough to understand and want more— my heart was ready to receive. I had already gotten to the point of appreciating the love of Christ and I understood the importance of being saved. I understood that all of this is what Jesus offered to anyone who would belive, and the Holy Spirit pointed that out to me. It was a point of change for me that I could have only experienced through the urging of the Holy Spirit.

That is one of the things that I love about the Holy Spirit: He finds pleasure in giving us insights into a deeper relationship with God. He gives us those insights through words that others have written or spoken, through experiences in which He highlights events that are or will occur, or through reading the Bible. He highlights key points that relate to our current situation, and will enhance our relationship with Him. It is understanding this truth about the relationship that matters a lot. Unlike what is depicted on TV and movies, He guides us into a relationship with the Lord that is so much deeper and more authentic than anything you can imagine. It's His privilege and honor to continue to woo us in the right direction, and to guide us to where we can have that encounter and relationship with the Lord on a regular basis. It is that truth about who the Lord truly is, that the Holy Spirit highlights. Also, the truth about how much He loves us, is what the Holy Spirit continues to convey to each and every one of us. In essence, the Holy Spirit is the **bridge of truth that highlights and connects us into the truth who is the Lord.**

As this chapter references worship, I'd like to take a moment to address what worship is. Worship is a word that is thrown around in many conversations with varying degrees of understanding. As I've mentioned to folks who I have ministered to over the years, there is a major misconception that—to them— worship is only slow music and lifting up their hands. The truth lies somewhere else, though. The outcome of worship can be music, lifting up hands, and singing; but worship is something even deeper than that. Worship is actually serving, and doing the will of the Lord willingly. Because of that relationship to the Lord, a person gladly serves Him and responds to His call. In that time of serving and communing with the Lord, an outward result is observed in the singing of music, lifting up of hands, dancing, and more. However, in order to truly worship the way that we are intended to worship, we have to have that connection through the Spirit of the Lord so that we are really understanding who, and what we are worshipping.

You see, people often want to worship something that they themselves have created. Many may worship a nice organization that they created to help folks in need, and they worship it because it brings great recognition to themselves. It gives the impression that they are a very caring and loving person. Yet, others will worship the image they create as a celebrity or a sports hero. That becomes an image that they worship, since it brings them notoriety. However, that really isn't the worship that we are called to. We're called to something much more; and in order to understand that worship, the Holy Spirit has to direct and show us the truth of what Jesus described as true worship.

There is a great account in the Bible about Jesus visiting a woman, in an area called Samaria.[30] They have this interesting conversation about worship where Jesus tells her that she didn't know what she was worshipping. He then proceeds to tell her that those who worship God, must worship Him in spirit and truth.[31] It's an interesting conversation because the woman never thought about the revelations that Jesus was giving; but Jesus was laying a template. A template that basically demonstrated that we must worship God in spirit because He is spirit. The only way that true worship can occur is through the enablement of the Holy Spirit. That Holy Spirit helps you understand the truth who is Jesus; and when you worship in spirit and in truth, you are now able to communicate, receive, and interact with the Lord on a regular basis. It is the Holy Spirit teaching us, speaking to us, urging us, and revealing to us, the truth and the way to go. He has a major role in the way we live today, but we just have to acknowledge it and abide by His direction.

The Holy Spirit will continue to urge us to learn of the Lord, and to remember the truth in which He spoke. He will spend time— should we allow him— to dictate and reveal to us who Jesus truly is, and why it is important for us to acknowledge and worship Him as the savior of the world. The Holy Spirit will also reveal to us our place in the plan of God. He continually teaches these things so that we know the real truth, not the limited perceived truth. The more of the truth that we learn and receive, the more that we grow into who we truly are in the Lord. The more that we spend time understanding through the Holy Spirit, the more that we have a grasp by the revelation of Jesus Christ. Once we understand that truth, then we become free in so many areas, that prior to, we were restrained and often imprisoned.

Going back to the statement of Pilate in John 18, I often wonder whether Pilate was earnestly trying to understand what truth really meant. Maybe he truly was trying to just understand everything that was happening, yet just could not get there. Maybe if he took more time, and did not relent to the will of those who were serving Jesus up for persecution, then maybe he might have begun the process of understanding truth; since the one who is the essence of truth was standing right in front of him. I wonder if there could have been a change in Pilate's life and trajectory? We will never know. As for us, however, we have to come to the understanding that the Holy Spirit is here to direct us to all truth: Jesus. Let me give you an example of how truth is revealed by using an event in the Bible.

Do you remember hearing (or reading) the account of Pentecost? You know the event where all of a sudden, the disciples came out of the room where they had been staying, and began speaking in other tongues? Many movies and books have been written about that event, and I'm sure you've heard some reference to it. However, even in that spectacular event, there is an example of truth working. If you read the account, you'll see that the Holy Spirit was the instigator of the event. Do you remember in Acts 2, where after they came out speaking in other tongues, everyone else who was in the city was astonished and asked themselves, 'What is this and what does it mean?' I can imagine that the confusion for those who were witnessing this event was high. I could also imagine many of them speaking amongst themselves asking questions about 'Who these people are,' and 'What is this that they're saying.' Since this type of manifestation had never occurred before, no one knew how to process it. It did not fit into a neat category that already existed. There was not a description that they could easily apply this event to. So, of course, they struggled to understand what was occurring. Eventually, as humans do, they began to draw their own conclusions— saying that the disciples were drunk. They began to laugh off what was a occurring, and to dismiss it. The reason why they dismissed it, was because they didn't understand it. They had no idea what was going on so, they relegated it to something unimportant.

When you read the Bible about this event, you see something happening shortly after people began to dismiss the event. The Bible clearly shows that Peter stood up with the other eleven disciples (meaning the other apostles who had been with Jesus) and began to speak to the crowd. This was after the Bible said they all were filled with the Holy Spirit. At this point, Peter began to teach the crowd the truth. He explains what happened and why this was a significant event. He spoke about words that the prophets had spoken about this event, and he conveyed to them the recent event of how they crucified Jesus. He said it in such a way that it brought conviction to the hearts of the listeners. Prior to this Pentecost event, I would attest that Peter really didn't have a full understanding of what was going on. Of his own knowledge and insight, he did not put all of the pieces together. However, when the Holy Spirit came (who is the one who will teach all things), it changed Peter's understanding so that he was now able to *understand and convey* the truth. He was able to do this because the Holy Spirit gave him the details of the truth and showed him how to communicate it to the crowd.

In that same manner, the Holy Spirit works in us today. How many of you would say that you really want to do the will of the Lord in your life? How many of you would say that if the Lord calls you, you will answer and do what He asked you to do? If that's you, then that is a form of worship when you do it. It's worshiping because you have an understanding of who the person is who is calling you. Since you understand who He is, you begin to appreciate the majesty and the depth of His call to you. That means, you're worshipping Him because of the truth that you know, and the revelation that the Spirit has given you.

Whenever we pursue the truth, the Holy Spirit is right there to reveal it to us, and to point us in the direction of the Lord. He will reveal more of the truth than you could have ever understood on your own. That is His job. We have to learn to let Him do His job in our lives. When we do, we will begin to notice Him speaking to us in every portion of our day, every portion of our week, and every portion of our months. It will grow into a continual conversation, if you allow it. Jesus sent the Holy Spirit to us for a purpose, so therefore, we need to take time to understand and to get to know what He is doing in our life.

Have you ever noticed that when you listen to someone minister or speak, they may have a similar cadence or method of preaching to many others; yet, there are some unique aspects about each person? Every person who may have trained under a famous minister will have similarities, but there are unique aspects (or gifts) that the Lord has given each person. They may have 80 to 90% of their teachers methods and mannerisms, but the final 10 to 20% is something that is uniquely theirs. What you also find, if you listen closely, is their revelation of the truth in the word of God, and the way in which they explain it, is unique to them. It is the same truth, but the depth of the revelation, and the method in which it is explained, is uniquely theirs. It comes from the time they spend with the Holy Spirit, and how He continues to reveal more and more truth to them about Jesus, and the plan that God has for each one of us. Those truths are limitless; and are only hindered by the amount of time we spend— or lack thereof— with the Holy Spirit.

Let me ask you now: Will you endeavour to spend more time listening and hearing the direction of the Spirit of

God? Even if you have built a solid relationship with the Holy Spirit, will you make it a part of your life to continue to make it stronger? The more you do, the deeper your revelation will be. The deeper your revelation is, the more of the truth you will understand. The more of the truth you understand, the more your life will be changed and enhanced. I hope you will deepen your relationship with the Holy Spirit in order to know how to worship in spirit and truth.

*F*or this reason I bow my knees to the Father of our Lord Jesus Christ, from whom the whole family in heaven and earth is named, that He would grant you, according to the riches of His glory, to be strengthened with might through His Spirit in the inner man,

Ephesians 3:14-16

The Enabler

Chapter 11

Have you ever felt like you need to do something for God, but you get tired just thinking about it; or better yet, maybe people have told you that you are destined for great things, but at the very thought of it, you feel overwhelmed? You see, part of the problem that we fall into, is that we often feel like we have to do it all by ourselves. Just the thought of the level of effort to address a problem or a situation, all in the name of God, can be overwhelming! If some of the most famous Christian leaders of the past had thought about the cost, or the effort involved to make a difference, they would never have done it. We have to keep in mind that it is not just us, but really, it is the Lord.

There is much that needs to be done on the earth today that I would categorize as 'Kingdom of God' business, but yet as the scriptures say, "The laborers are few."[32] I believe that there are a few reasons why there are few laborers. One of those reason is that people count the cost before they even begin to say 'yes' to the calling. They realize the energy or time that it will take; and many become fearful of the price of achieving that effort. They become adverse to how saying 'yes' to the Lord could potentially alter their own plans. They, instead, would rather continue as they are. This mode of thinking completely neglects the most important factor: the Lord. He never calls us to do something that we cannot achieve through Him.

This is why I enjoy the verse listed at the beginning of this chapter. When Paul wrote this particular verse. he had a specific goal in mind. Although I acknowledge his goal, when I personally read it, I realize that the Holy Spirit is there to enable and help me achieve the goals that I must achieve (of course they are directly received from Him). He serves as not only the teacher, but also the enabler. That means, He provides strength for us, since He knows that we are weak in, and of, ourselves. He provides us with the fortitude to keep going when we want to give up. He allows us to continue to push forward, even when it seems like all is lost.

Like before, I have a few examples to better illustrate my point. Do you remember Samson[33] from the Bible? Think about all the tremendous feats that he did. What about Elijah?[34] Do you remember the moment in the Bible where after he had defeated all the prophets of Baal, how he outran the chariot? There was even the account of Phillip.[35] Do you recall how after he evangelized to the Ethiopian eunuch, he all of a sudden wasn't there, and was found miles away? These are just a few simple examples of how the Holy Spirit enables people to do incredible and marvelous things; but we also know that God is no respector of person. Therefore, He can, and will, enable you with the strength needed to achieve your purpose.

Have you ever watched a football game where the quarterback hands off the ball to the running back, and as soon as the running back touches the ball, the defenders are all over him? For the average running back, it would be considered a dead play.[36] However, when you have a special or star player, it's never over until it really is over. On so many occassions, I've seen elite players make yardage when it seems like it would be impossible. There may be defenders all around them— possibly trying to tackle them— but somehow, some way, they elude them all; and are still able to make yardage going forward.

The enabler, the Holy Spirit, works similarly. He allows us to be a star athlete on any field. He allows us to be able to do whatever is necessary to get things done. Let me give you a simple and practical example. Years ago, one of the many things that I had shared with my wife was that I had always wanted to ride all the way up to Maine. I don't know why I really wanted to ride to Maine, but all of a sudden this goal just seemed to be inside of me. I wanted to go all the way up to the top just to say that I went all the way to the border of Canada via Maine. This trek would, by no means, be easy as I live in the mid-Atlantic. This means that a trip like that is very long, and it is easily equivalent to going to Florida by car. However, since this goal was deep inside of me for whatever reason, I asked the Lord to help me make this drive. You see, I've covered many miles over the years, especially when my kids were small. Even though I like to drive now, it's always a mental challenge because as soon as I start the trip, I'm not as excited about the drive as I was planning the trip. So, I have to encourage myself to push forward.

Thankfully, I made the drive all the way up to Maine with my wife as co-pilot. Since I was so insterested in making this trip, I decided that I definitely wanted to drive the whole way. I won't lie, there were parts on the way going up, where I was tired and was losing interest; but when that occured I did ask the Holy Spirit to help me to reach this goal. Again, I'm not sure why it was such a big deal, but once I have something in mind, I feel like I have to do it. Since I hadn't driven that far in a number of years, I definitely needed the help and enablement that comes from the Holy Spirit. What I found out was, every time I was starting to lose interest because the drive was taking so long, I would feel this surge of energy that would come through to keep me going. Needless to say, we made the trip all the way up to about the Canadian border, at the farthest point of Maine. We spent a couple of days riding around to look at Maine's scenery, and then drove all the way back. To most, that's not a good idea of a trip, but it was a road trip that I wanted to take; and a trip that I wanted to successfully drive. If you ask me if I want to do it again the same way? I would answer, not at all. It was just a desire, goal, and achievement that I wanted to have.

The Holy Spirit works in all of your lives the same way, when you allow Him to. For example: If someone calls and says that they need you to help with a business event or a church event or anything else, but you feel as though you don't have the skill set or capability, you need to lean in and ask the Holy Spirit for the guidance and enablement to succeed. It doesn't matter the venue, if this is something towards your calling or the responsibility that you have, He will allow you to do it.

If you are a parent, or have ever observed parents, you realize that if they have active children, their hands are always full. Most have to work to raise their kids effectively. There are countless times as parents where you feel exhausted and unable to keep moving forward; but it is through the grace of the Lord, and the enablement of the Holy Spirit, that all parents are able to successfully do everything that's needed.

As it relates to the Holy Spirit's speaking, He is the enabler to cause us to speak truth and wisdom at the perfect time. He gives us the ability to articulate topics, thoughts, and revelations that we in and of ourselves would never know or understand. He does this in order to communicate truth to those who need to hear it. Even in the Old Testament, Moses aknowledged that he was not a good speaker; in response the Lord appointed Aaron to help Moses. In a much more perfect way, the Holy Spirit is the one that teaches us what to say, at the moment it needs to be said.

Think about this for a moment. If the Holy Spirit enables— or teaches— us what to say, that means He is communicating with us. When I refer to communication, I mean the transfer, or the relation, of knowledge. In order to transfer knowledge, you have to utilize communication in some way, like speaking. That means the Holy Spirit will speak to us, and through us, at the appropriate times. If there is a time where the Gospel needs to be explained, you may find yourself speaking or explaining it in a simplistic, yet powerful way that others would be able to grasp the truth you are articulating.

Have you ever noticed that some preachers have a way of just impacting you when you hear them speak? When you stop and truly analyze the situation, you realize that they, in and of themselves, may not be the best preachers or teachers; but somehow, when they minister, their words have such a powerful impact on you. In most cases, it is the Holy Spirit using that vessel— or person— to communicate to you in a way that you can receive. That same person that you received so well, may not be the appropriate one to preach to your neighbor. Your neighbor may need another type of person, or method, to communicate the truths that are located in the word of God.

What made Billy Graham such an effective preacher? I believe it was the way the Holy Spirit moved through him, and spoke through him, that allowed Billy Graham to explain the Bible in such a simplistic way; making it easier for the Gospel to be received by thousands and thousands and thousands of people. The way that the Holy Spirit used him, allowed for most people to be able to receive what he preached. However, Billy Graham still could not reach everybody. What made Kenneth Hagin so effective? It wasn't his degrees or level of education, but I would suggest that it was the Holy Spirit of God working through him. There have been generations of people that he affected, and is still impacting, even though he has gone home to be with the Lord. He was able to deliver truth based on the revelation the Holy Spirit gave him, and the way the Holy Spirit used it. Both of these are small samples of great men and women who preached the word effectively, because the Holy Spirit used— and still uses— them, *and* they allowed all the Spirit to move through them. What about you? You may be the next best communicator of the Gospel, but you have to allow the Holy Spirit to work through you. He does speak to you, and He will fill your mouth with the words to speak at the appropriate times.

One of the privileges that I've had over time, is to train those who are aspiring to be ministers of the Gospel. Whenever I work with folks and trained them, I have to spend time looking at their hearts (via the Holy Spirit's guidance). One of the key things that we all must have, whether we are called for a five-fold ministry or some other serving capacity, is we should have a heart for God. When I look at the heart, I see several things.

Some have a loving and emotional attachment for the Lord, but not a good understanding. Others have a commitment to worship the Lord, but not necessarily to serve Him. What I mean by that is, when it comes to actually keeping His commands, and doing the things that He asks of them, they are not very interested. Instead, they are only interested in preaching— or telling others— what the Bible says, but not necessarily living by the Bible themselves. As you might expect, I spend time highlighting those aspects, with the hopes that they would understand and reap a more fulfilling relationship and ministry.

Once they are aware of the need for a deeper relationship with the Holy Spirit, then I can proceed to teach them how to be used by the Lord. The Lord will provide the enablement to teach, minister, and guide, based on His Holy Spirit. I stress that the Holy Spirit will give them the right words to say, at the right time. It has to be Him. Some may try to set up the most detailed outline or plan for how they *think* everything will go. Yet, they are the ones who often find that while they are delivering a message, or teaching a lesson, the Holy Spirit changes the whole situation in order to push them and guide them in a direction they did not anticipate. I enjoy those moments because I'm always interested to find out if they will follow the moving of the Holy Spirit, or if they will stick heavily to their outlined plan. From my experience, those that have stuck heavily to the outlined plan have finished successfully, but not with the impact that they could have had.

On the other hand, those that just wait for the Spirit to fill their mouth run into another issue. The issue with this type of person is they still need to spend time with the Lord, and commune with Him, so that they are in the right alignment with His will for that speaking opportunity. When people do not spend any prep time, they often fall into the trap of repeating the same topic, and the same instances over and over again. Yes, the Holy Spirit can speak through a person— and He often does— but that person still needs to have a relationship with Him in order to understand what needs to be done right at that moment. The Lord orchestrates everything for His church through His Spirit, and we must make sure that we are in tune with the Lord's will.

Let me close this chapter by encouraging you. I understand that the Bible says the laborers are few, but as it applies to you, let's hope that you are counted as one of those laborers who have answered the call. He so longs for you to be active in the affairs of the Kingdom of God. Please don't spend time counting the cost or the effort, but depend fully on the enablement of the Holy Spirit. If you look at it from that perspective, then you will want to say 'yes.' Understand that anything that is worthwhile, He will provide for you. Don't think about potential losses, but understand the potential gains. Everything that you will gain is everlasting through answering 'yes' to the call. Just know, without a doubt, He will enable you to do all things. Therefore, there should be nothing to hinder you from doing the will of God in your life. I hope you agree.

The Lord Jesus Christ be with your spirit. Grace be with you. Amen.

2 Timothy 4:22

Amen

Chapter 12

You've made it to this last chapter of the book! I am so glad that you stuck with it. Hopefully, you are understanding more about the Holy Spirit and how He speaks. He is an invaluable Person to have in your life. Jesus said that He would send one like Him, and He has done just as He said. So, in light of that, I decided to call this chapter "Amen."[37] Amen means "it is so." In this chapter, I am affirming— based on my own experiences— that what Jesus said about the Holy Spirit, is actually true. Let me take a moment to tell you about some personal encounters that I didn't allude to earlier in the book. I am not sharing anything about the Holy Spirit that I haven't experienced myself. I have really enjoyed getting to know the Holy Spirit more and more with each passing day, and I look forward to an eternity more with the Spirit of God. You see, this experience is a constant experience. One which gets better and better the more time we spend together.

The first encounter that I had with the Holy Spirit— at least to my understanding— was during salvation. I had come to a point (at an early age) that I began to yearn for more of the Lord. Not the ritualistic type of encounter that I had grown up around, but a real "knowing." There was an instance where I was watching a Christian children's program, and I heard the speaker say, "Come unto the Lord." The speaker then proceeded to talk about how much the Lord loved me, and how He paid the price on the cross so that I would be free. He even spoke a bit more about the importance of salvation through Jesus. It was at that moment, that I felt this deep pull inside of me to respond. I was in the room by myself, but the television was on. The person speaking on the television, spoke in such a way that the words penetrated deep inside of my being. It was such a deep call and pull, that I responded with tears streaming down my face. That was my moment of salvation. I began to realize little by little, although I didn't truly understand everything, that it was the Holy Spirit pulling me to answer the call of the Lord.

Since that time, I have had countless encounters with the Holy Spirit. At first, it was more urgings (or a 'sense') that I should do something. As time went on, I began to notice numerous times when I read the Bible, that it seemed like words were highlighted for me. It seemed that the words which were illuminated, were phrases and verses that were important to what I was going through (or dealing with) at that moment. It was if He painted the answers right in the Bible just for me. I used to get amazed at how this worked, because the sections (or words) in the Bible that I was reading and were highlighted to me, were sections that I had read before; yet, they now contained a 'new' meaning. It was at that moment that they seem to resonate and illuminate so that I could actually understand what I needed to do at that time.

Later, as I progressed in this relationship, I began to realize that while I was praying about various situations or people, scriptures would rise up inside of me as if they were answering the prayer that I was praying. The first time, I thought it was strange and that I was imagining thing; but as time went on, these occurrences continued to happen. My response began to change into one of wonder and awe. As I thought more about what was happening, I realized something. The scripture verses that were being revealed to me, were ones I may have read or even memorized years prior. I often forgot that I had read those versus, but they were appropriate for that particular situation.

When the Bible verses arose from within, it was not ritualistic or rigid. The way they would arise was the verses being woven throughout my prayers. Initially, it would be almost as if a billboard was put in front of my eyes, and I could recite the verses from them. Afterwards, just to be certain, I would go and research what I saw. When I did, I would notice what I saw would match exactly to a particular set of verses in the Bible. It would be the answer to what I was praying. It was amazing!

Yet still, that wasn't the end of it. I still wanted more. As my desire to grow increased, I continued to pursue the Lord and listen to the Spirit of the Lord as He directed me. What began to happen next really astonished me. Not only was I seeing the verses while I was praying, but then I began to hear as well as see the verses. In a Spirit to spirit communication, I would begin to hear those verses quoted. At first, it startled me. I didn't know what to make of it. Initially, I would think that I heard something strange from outside or on a television in my home, yet when I looked around no one else was around. When I proceeded to look up what I heard, I found out that it was really scripture. I realized it truly was the Holy Spirit teaching me that the truth is in the Word.

One thing you should know is, many years prior to this level of relationship with the Holy Spirit, I spent time regularly reading the Bible. This was something I chose to do, because I wanted to understand the basics. At the church I was attending at the time, there were many wonderful, loving, and faithful people. The challenge was, we learned very high-level, superficial Christianity, but I longed for more. Therefore, I embarked on the journey of reading it from cover to cover. What I didn't realize was, those verses were being placed in my spiritual "well" to be used at a later time. It's from that "well" that the Holy Spirit pulled the verses to answer my prayers.

As you can imagine, these revelations, encounters, and developments were somewhat unusual. So, I began to ask myself if these situations were Biblical. Fortunately, I realized the answer was "YES!" Because I was trying to understand more of what the Lord had promised, and I was pursuing Him, these encounters and revelations were able to occur— and still are occurring. It felt strange for much of the time, since there were not many people around me who could relate to the things that I was experiencing; but over time, I realized that it was normal to experience these things when you pursue the Lord. As I grew even closer to the Lord, my growth continued. Because of this, years later, I had experiences where I could hear the audible voice of the Spirit of the Lord calling me. One night in particular, I heard His voice so loud, that I jumped out of the bed and looked to see if my wife heard. She was sound asleep! However, I knew it was the Spirit of the Lord, because it resonated all the way through my very being. At that moment in life, I needed to pray about some things *and* I needed some answers at that time, and He was responding to those needs.

This was similar to the experience the Prophet Samuel had when he was a young boy.[38] Samuel, who was dedicated to serving the Lord at a young age by his mother, was lying in the bed at night when he heard the Lord call him. It happened three times, but it wasn't until the fourth time that Samuel realized it was the Lord. Samuel heard his name called so clearly, yet no one else heard it. It is amazing how the Lord can direct His conversation to whomever He wants, without anyone else hearing. He works the same way today. I can't tell you that this happens every minute of every day, but from time to time in this relationship, I do experience this type of interaction. I can still be startled, depending on the tone and urgency of His calling; but without a doubt, His voice is clear and direct. You too can experience a relationship like this— or even better— based on your desire to pursue the truths that the Lord has laid out about the Holy Spirit. You can build that relationship so that He can reveal more about who you are intended to be in Him, and how He wants you to impact the community.

Let me share one other area where your relationship with the Holy Spirit can manifest. Some of you already have a strong and deeply rooted understanding of who the Holy Spirit is. Undoubtedly, you have developed this relationship over the course of your life; but you have probably also experienced situations where the Holy Spirit tells you things in advance. You may hear Him audibly, or see a message visually, or just have a "knowing" inside as if a Spirit to spirit download had occurred. I'm not speaking of a fortune teller that you see on street corners or anything like that (that is against what the Lord is talking about here). What we are the sharing is the Holy Spirit's ability to let you see things that may occur. These things can be beneficial, or they could be warnings of things that might occur.

For example, several years ago during the month of August, I was walking inside my house toward the front door. And like most homes, we have windows at the front of our house. Although I only glanced outside the window for a moment, it was almost as if I froze in place for a period of time. While gazing outside, I saw a vision. Even though it was August and the temperature was very hot with the sun shining brightly, I was transported months ahead and all I saw was heavy snowfall. I felt as though I was in the same spot, in the same house, but at a different time period. I stood gazing outside the window, but yet, I saw something different than what was actually occurring outside. Instead of the bright sunshine, the green grass, the birds flying through the air, and warm temperatures, I was seeing snow fall. Not light snow, but very heavy snow. The ground was already covered with several inches of snow, and large flakes were still falling. The leaves had already fallen from the trees, and there were very few birds to be seen. Instead of feeling the heat and the warmth from a hot August day, I felt the cool of a cold December day. As I stood there for a moment, I was trying to understand what I was seeing. After a few moments of this (I can't tell you for sure how long I was standing there, but it felt like a very long time), I came to an understanding. At that point in my relationship with the Holy Spirit, I realized that it was an indication— or a warning— that we would have a major snowstorm when winter arrived. When you receive that type of warning, you have to ask yourself what it is that you are supposed to do? Well, I knew that the Holy Spirit was telling me to get all of my winter gear prepared. So, I made sure that I had boots, a snow thrower, a shovel, salt for the sidewalks, wood for the fireplace, and everything else that I could possibly need. In addition, I made sure the winter machinery was serviced and functioning.

Fast forward to several months later, during the winter, we had a major snowstorm. Thanks to the Holy Spirit's warning, I was prepared and everything we needed was in place. If I'm not mistaken, we had multiple snowstorms that year. Just think if I had brushed off that vision. What would have happened if I did not pay any attention to it? I would've been struggling during the midst of a heavy storm. My snow throwers may not have functioned; or I may not have had all of the supplies nor the outerwear that was necessary. This is a simple, but practical example. The Holy Spirit often deals in practical areas, but we just have to listen.

Do you have examples of when the Holy Spirit worked this way in your life? Have you ignored Him? What were the consequences? I hope you have learned, just like I have, that He is always working for your best interest. He is trying to teach us, so we should strive to be the best students we can be.

Although this book does not answer every question that you could possibly have about the Holy Spirit, it is a good start. My hope in writing this book is that it will profoundly impact you, and cause you to consider the truth about the Spirit of God. If you begin to read the Word more, and apply the teachings to your life— especially as He speaks about the Holy Spirit— my time spent writing this book will be worth it. I guarantee you that if you begin to seek the Lord fully, the Holy Spirit will be right there to teach and encourage you about everything the Lord has promised. That is His role. He knows how you learn, and the best way to cause you to retain what is said. He will set up "courses" for you, so that you will understand and graduate from glory to glory. However, it's only through understanding and seeking the Lord through the Bible, that you will begin to know the truth.

Finally, I want to assure you that the Holy Spirit is there for you no matter where you live or what you look like. There is no particular image of the type of person that you have to appear as in order to understand the truths that are written in the Bible. You just have to pursue Him, and He will cause you to be everything that He designed you to be. Will you take that *leap* and be a part of this journey? Will you grow from glory to glory in order to begin to utilize all of what the Lord has given you? I hope your answer is 'yes' because the Holy Spirit is speaking— right now.

Endnotes

1   "Spirit of the Living God" is a 1926 hymn by Daniel Iverson. Daniel Iverson wrote the first stanza and tune of this hymn after hearing a sermon on the Holy Spirit during an evangelism crusade by the George Stephans Evangelistic Team in Orlando, Florida, 1926. The hymn was sung at the crusade and then printed in leaflets for use at other services. Published anonymously in Robert H. Coleman's Revival Songs (1929) with alterations in the tune, this short hymn gained much popularity by the middle of the century. Since the 1960s it has again been properly credited to Iverson.

2   The term describes dancing, shaking or other boisterous movements by church attendees who perceive themselves as being under the influence of the Holy Spirit. Holy Rolling is sometimes used derisively by those outside these denominations, as if to describe people literally rolling on the floor in an uncontrolled manner.

3   But the Advocate, the Holy Spirit, whom the Father will send in my name, will teach you all things and will remind you of everything I have said to you. (John 14:26)

4   The New King James Version. (1982). (Jn 3:5–8). Nashville: Thomas Nelson.

5   Pharisees were teachers of the Hebrew Law and influential during Jesus' time. They were distinguished by a strict observance of the traditional and written law, and most commonly held to have pretensions to superior sanctity.

6   ...the Spirit of truth. The world cannot accept him, because it neither sees him nor knows him. But you know him, for he lives with you and will be in you (John 14:17 NIV).

7 Baptism of Jesus

8   But the Advocate, the Holy Spirit, whom the Father will send in my name, will teach you all things and will remind you of everything I have said to you. (John 14:26 NIV)

9   Now the earth was formless and empty, darkness was

over the surface of the deep, and the Spirit of God was hovering over the waters. (Genesis 1:2 NIV)

10   But the Helper (Comforter, Advocate, Intercessor— Counselor, Strengthener, Standby), the Holy Spirit, whom the Father will send in My name [in My place, to represent Me and act on My behalf], He will teach you all things. And He will help you remember everything that I have told you. (John 14:26). And I will ask the Father, and He will give you another [a]Helper (Comforter, Advocate, Intercessor—Counselor, Strengthener, Standby), to be with you forever— the Spirit of Truth, whom the world cannot receive [and take to its heart] because it does not see Him or know Him, but you know Him because He (the Holy Spirit) remains with you continually and will be in you. (John 14:16-17 NIV)

11   Omnipresent— everywhere (present) at the same time.

12   In the beginning [before all time] was the Word (Christ), and the Word was with God, and the Word was God Himself. (John 1:1)

13   The Holy Spirit would come in Jesus' name and authority as a distinct Person. He came to teach all things, in order for us to understand all that Jesus' ministry and teachings were about. While He is here to teach, as John 14:26 dictates, He is also here to help us remember all that we've been taught.

14   "For God so [greatly] loved and dearly prized the world, that He [even] gave His [One and] [a]only begotten Son, so that whoever believes and trusts in Him [as Savior] shall not perish, but have eternal life. (John 3:16 AMP)

15   "But now I am going to Him who sent Me; and none of you asks Me, 'Where are You going?' But because I have said these things to you, sorrow has filled your hearts [and taken complete possession of them]. But I tell you the truth, it is to your advantage that I go away; for if I do not go away, the [a]Helper (Comforter, Advocate, Intercessor—Counselor, Strengthener, Standby) will not come to you; but if I go, I will send Him (the Holy Spirit) to you [to be in close fellowship with you]. And He, when He comes, will convict the world about [the guilt of] sin [and the need for a Savior], and about righteousness,

and about judgment: about sin [and the true nature of it], because they do not believe in Me [and My message]; about righteousness [personal integrity and godly character], because I am going to My Father and you will no longer see Me; about judgment [the certainty of it], because the ruler of this world (Satan) has been judged and condemned. "I have many more things to say to you, but you cannot bear [to hear] them now. But when He, the Spirit of Truth, comes, He will guide you into all the truth [full and complete truth]. For He will not speak on His own initiative, but He will speak whatever He hears [from the Father—the message regarding the Son], and He will disclose to you what is to come [in the future]. He will glorify and honor Me, because He (the Holy Spirit) will take from what is Mine and will disclose it to you. All things that the Father has are Mine. Because of this I said that He [the Spirit] will take from what is Mine and will reveal it to you. (John 16: 5-15 AMP)

16   For what person knows the thoughts and motives of a man except the man's spirit within him? So also no one knows the thoughts of God except the Spirit of God. (1 Corinthians 2:11)

17   Grace is the unmerited (unearned) favor of God toward man(kind).

18   In 1 Samuel 16, we find that God has instructed the prophet Samuel to anoint a new king of Israel. He points out the household that the new king should be chosen from, and tells Samuel to go and anoint the new king. Samuel obeys the Lord and goes. Once Samuel arrives and sees the sons that Jesse has provided, he is sure of himself that one of these sons must be the new king. Each one—by man's standards— fit the vision of what a king should look like and carry themselves, however, the Lord had other plans. God specifically tells Samuel that He doesn't look at the outward appearance, but at a person's heart. A heart for God was most important Him. Through this reasoning, David was brought in from the field where he was tending sheep and playing music, to stand before Samuel— then he was promptly anointed. The Bible takes extra care to mention that when David was anointed, the Spirit of God came upon him. Although,

Samuel poured the oil on his head, it was just a symbol of this inward reality (the Spirit resting in him).

19   The Holy Spirit can be grieved. (Ephesians 4:29-32) The Spirit of God wants what's best for us; and what is best for us is life. When we do things opposite of what God intends (or that is out of live with the will of God), it can grieve the Holy Spirit. Life is any and everything in God, so what is outside of that is not life, but death. Since Jesus came so that we may have life, and have life more abundantly (John 10:10); opposing everything that Jesus— as the Holy Spirit always points to Jesus— is grieves the Holy Spirit. Things like disobedience, bitterness, living in fear, and more.

20   The Apostle Paul wrote much of the New Testament. He was, originally, named Saul but was renamed after his encounter with Christ on the Damascus Road. He was born a Roman citizen to Jewish parents, and was well learned; having studied the Torah extensively— becoming something of a Pharisee. His overzealous piousness is what turns him to persecuting the followers of Jesus in Judea and Jerusalem. He then has is encounter with Christ and completely turns his life around; instead, preaching of Jesus Christ's divinity.

21   You ask [God for something] and do not receive it, because you ask with wrong motives [out of selfishness or with an unrighteous agenda], so that [when you get what you want] you may spend it on your [hedonistic] desires. (James 4:2-3 AMP)

22   In Acts 13, we see Paul and Barnabus are commissioned by the Holy Spirit to become missionaries. Through fasting and prayer, they were able hear the the specific direction that the Lord wanted them to go in. Through their willingness and obedience to the Lord, they were able to minister to countless people, even the Roman Proconsul in Paphos (a proconsul was esponsible for an entire province and answered to the Roman Senate). Here, the proconsul even asked for them to tell him the Gospel. While ministering to the proconsul, a sorcerer tried to dissuade the him from learning of the Gospel; however, this turned into an opportunity as the Holy Spirit used Paul to

pronouce judgement directly over the sorcerer. The sorcerer immediately went blind, and this caused the proconsul to belive in Christ.

23   The Church at Antioch was crucial for many reasons. First, they were a mixed church, with both Jews andGentiles being members. Second, it is here that the followers of the Gospel were first called Christians. Third, Antioch was the capital of the Roman province of Syria and Phoenicia. Since the city was set on the Orontes River, they were able to have a port. During Paul's day Antioch was the third largest city in the Roman empire, only paling in comparison to Rome and Alexandria. Antioch was also the place where Herod the Great paved over 2 miles (3km) of its streets with marble. Antioch also became one of the four great centers of the Christian faith before the Council of Nicaea in 325AD.

24   The thief comes only to steal and kill and destroy; I have come that they may have life, and have it to the full. (John 10:10 NIV)

25   To be 'Born Again' doesn't mean to physically re-enter your mother's womb in and be rebirthed, much like Nicodemus thought (John 3). Instead, being born again refers to the new beginning in the relationship between God and the one who is 'born again' (John 3:3, 7). It is through this transformation, this new beginning, that we are adopted by God, through Jesus Christ (Romans 8:15, 16; Galatians 4:5; 1 John 3:1). Similar to those who are legally adopted in our world, they experience a change of status, becoming part of God's family (2 Corinthians 6:18). Once adopted, everything that is God, is now ours, by right.

26   To 'open your heart' or to 'open the eyes of your heart' means to readily and willingly give up control of oneself in order to be used for God's calling. Opening our heart to God and His will, helps us in many ways. First, we become teachable. Since the Holy Spirit is meant to teach us all things, becoming someone that's teachable should be our first step towards a closer relationship with the Lord. Second, it gives us a testimony. When our eyes are opened to the wonderful, miraculous, and excellent things of the Lord (and what He's done for us), we begin to

develop our own testimony. Having a testimony is crucial in your Christian walk. When we have a testimony— and we really want more of the Lord in our lives— we desire to tell others about it. When we tell others about how good God has been to us (and in our lives), then we are bearing witness to Christ. When we bear witness to Christ, others will inadvertently be drawn to Him. Lastly, we can consistently converse with the Holy Spirit. The more we talk to Him, the more we develop a deeper relationship with Him. When we develop a deeper relationship with the Holy Spirit, we begin to understand the will of the Lord for our lives and our communities— this directly effects our surroundings. So, opening our hearts' eyes to the things of God through studying the Bible, prayer, and the Christian fellowship is necessary for our daily Christian walk.

27   A temple is a place of worship; or where God dwells.

28   A layleader is a member of the laity in a congregation who has been chosen as a leader either by their peers or the leadership of the congregation. Some denominations will allow a lay leader to perform all of the duties of an ordained minister, except in cases where the State requires ordination.

29   Pontius Pilate was a Roman governor of Judea during the reign of Emperor Tiberius. Not much is known about Pilate, however, since he was elected to governorship, it is assumed that he came from a wealthy and powerful family with possible connections to the Emperor himself. It is also assumed that he had previous military and administrative experience. His most notable (and most known) role, however, was his approval of Jesus' crucifixion.

30   The major issue between the Jews and the Samaritans was that they disagreed about where God's people should worship. This disagreement led to years of enmity between the two peoples. The enmity was so strong, that Jews would go out of their way to pass around Samaria when traveling (going through Samaria would make their journey shorter).

31   "God is Spirit, and those who worship Him must worship in spirit and truth." (John 4:24 NIV)

32   Jesus went through all the towns and villages, teaching

in their synagogues, proclaiming the good news of the kingdom and healing every disease and sickness. When he saw the crowds, he had compassion on them, because they were harassed and helpless, like sheep without a shepherd. Then he said to his disciples, "The harvest is plentiful but the workers are few. 38 Ask the Lord of the harvest, therefore, to send out workers into his harvest field. (Matthew 9:35-38)

33   Then Samson reached toward the two central pillars on which the temple stood. Bracing himself against them, his right hand on the one and his left hand on the other, Samson said, "Let me die with the Philistines!" Then he pushed with all his might, and down came the temple on the rulers and all the people in it. Thus he killed many more when he died than while he lived. Then his brothers and his father's whole family went down to get him. They brought him back and buried him between Zorah and Eshtaol in the tomb of Manoah his father. He had led[a] Israel twenty years. (Judges 16:29-31 NIV)

34   The seventh time the servant reported, "A cloud as small as a man's hand is rising from the sea." So Elijah said, "Go and tell Ahab, 'Hitch up your chariot and go down before the rain stops you.'" Meanwhile, the sky grew black with clouds, the wind rose, a heavy rain started falling and Ahab rode off to Jezreel. The power of the Lord came on Elijah and, tucking his cloak into his belt, he ran ahead of Ahab all the way to Jezreel. (1 Kings 18:44-46 NIV)

35   When they came up out of the water, the Spirit of the Lord suddenly took Philip away, and the eunuch did not see him again, but went on his way rejoicing. Philip, however, appeared at Azotus and traveled about, preaching the gospel in all the towns until he reached Caesarea. (Acts 8:39-10 NIV)

36   In gridiron football, a dead ball is a condition that occurs between football plays, after one of the following has occurred:

1.   The player with the ball runs out of bounds.
2.   The player with the ball is downed, either by being tackled to the ground or by deliberately downing himself (also known as 'taking a knee').
3.   A forward pass touches the ground or travels out of

bounds without being caught (an incomplete pass).

4. Any kick travels out of bounds and/or hits the goal post or crossbar in flight.

5. The ball is fumbled out of bounds.

6. A scoring play occurs.

37   Amen means 'it is so.' The Hebrew word Emunah, from which Amen shares its roots, means faith. However, it's not just any faith. The word, Emunah, carries more than just faith, but a certainty and steadfastness that comes from continually realizing (or encountering) God's faithfulness. It is eluding to a life fully reliant upon the Lord. This means so much more when you realize that the word, Amen, was used in a much more binding and legal way durng Jesus' time— almost like a signature (legal reprocussions could apply). When we say 'Amen' to close out a prayer, it is not a ritual with no power. Instead, it is an agreement to act upon what we have prayed.

38   The boy Samuel ministered before the Lord under Eli. In those days the word of the Lord was rare; there were not many visions. One night Eli, whose eyes were becoming so weak that he could barely see, was lying down in his usual place. The lamp of God had not yet gone out, and Samuel was lying down in the house of the Lord, where the ark of God was. Then the Lord called Samuel. Samuel answered, "Here I am." And he ran to Eli and said, "Here I am; you called me." But Eli said, "I did not call; go back and lie down." So he went and lay down. Again the Lord called, "Samuel!" And Samuel got up and went to Eli and said, "Here I am; you called me." "My son," Eli said, "I did not call; go back and lie down." Now Samuel did not yet know the Lord: The word of the Lord had not yet been revealed to him. A third time the Lord called, "Samuel!" And Samuel got up and went to Eli and said, "Here I am; you called me." Then Eli realized that the Lord was calling the boy. So Eli told Samuel, "Go and lie down, and if he calls you, say, 'Speak, Lord, for your servant is listening.'" So Samuel went and lay down in his place. The Lord came and stood there, calling as at the other times, "Samuel! Samuel!" Then Samuel said, "Speak, for your servant is listening." And the Lord said to Samuel: "See, I am about to

do something in Israel that will make the ears of everyone who hears about it tingle. At that time I will carry out against Eli everything I spoke against his family—from beginning to end. For I told him that I would judge his family forever because of the sin he knew about; his sons blasphemed God, and he failed to restrain them. Therefore I swore to the house of Eli, 'The guilt of Eli's house will never be atoned for by sacrifice or offering.'" Samuel lay down until morning and then opened the doors of the house of the Lord. He was afraid to tell Eli the vision, 16 but Eli called him and said, "Samuel, my son." Samuel answered, "Here I am." "What was it he said to you?" Eli asked. "Do not hide it from me. May God deal with you, be it ever so severely, if you hide from me anything he told you." So Samuel told him everything, hiding nothing from him. Then Eli said, "He is the Lord; let him do what is good in his eyes." The Lord was with Samuel as he grew up, and he let none of Samuel's words fall to the ground. And all Israel from Dan to Beersheba recognized that Samuel was attested as a prophet of the Lord. The Lord continued to appear at Shiloh, and there he revealed himself to Samuel through his word. (1 Samuel 3 NIV)